John Aspinwall Hodge
Recognition after Death
ISBN/EAN: 9783337404437
Printed in Europe, USA, Canada, Australia, Japan
Cover: Foto ©Lupo / pixelio.de

More available books at **www.hansebooks.com**

Books of Devotion and Consolation.

Come Ye Apart. Daily Readings in the Life of Christ.
    By the Rev. J. R. Miller, D.D $1.50
The Bow in the Cloud. Macduff 50
Wells of Baca. Macduff 50
Clarke's Scripture Promises 50
Bogatzky's Golden Treasury. Gilt edges 75
The Empty Crib. By Dr. Cuyler. Gilt edges . . . 1.00
God's Light on Dark Clouds. By Dr. Cuyler 75
Smith's Daily Remembrancer. Gilt edges. . . . 1.00
Macduff's Family Prayers 1.00
Macduff's Morning Family Prayers for a Year . . . 2.00
Macduff's Morning and Night Watches 50
Macduff's Mind and Words of Jesus. Red edges . . .50
Words of Comfort for Bereaved Parents. Logan . . 1.00
Shoes of Peace. By Anna B. Warner 75
Private Devotion. By Hannah More 50
The Pathway of Promise 50
Morning by Morning. By Spurgeon 1.00
Evening by Evening. By Spurgeon. 1.00

ROBERT CARTER AND BROTHERS.

Recognition After Death

BY THE

REV. J. ASPINWALL HODGE, D. D.

PREFACE.

As a pastor, I have found persons doubting the possibility of the recognition of souls after death. The thought of heaven was therefore less attractive to them than it should be, and the idea of reunion brought no consolation when they were mourning the death of loved ones. The separation seemed to them unending. I have been surprised that very many, while believing the precious truth, are anxious to learn upon what grounds it rests, and by what means the recognition is to be secured. At present the Christian public is much interested in every question which involves the state of the soul after death. Many excellent books have been written on the general subject, but few of these do more than touch upon recognition. I therefore send forth this little book, designed to show that we shall hereafter see and know each other, praying that it may bring comfort and new anticipations to many who are sorrowing over the separations which death is accomplishing in their home circles.

J. A. H.

Hartford, Conn., 1889.

RECOGNITION AFTER DEATH.

I.

IMMORTALITY AND RECOGNITION.

THE immortality of the soul has always been very generally admitted. There is a real difference between mind and matter, soul and body. We are spiritual persons, for a time dwelling in the flesh. Our bodies, with their many infirmities, are recognized as great hindrances—our physical faculties are too few, and too imperfect to satisfy our desires. We long for clearer and wider vision, more perfect hearing, and more rapid means of transportation. These aspirations lead to manifold inventions in all ages and places. The short space, during which our bodies can stand the wear and tear of this spiritual activity, and the increasing infirmities of the flesh, produce an almost universal conviction that, however dependent our souls may now be on our bodies, they can and must continue to live after "the dust returns to the earth as it was."[1] This is not merely a general hope. It is an instinct of human nature, which produces an assurance alike in the savage and in the civilized, in the heathen and in those taught by revelation, and in all ages and under all circumstances. Ancient mythologies and all forms of modern true and false religions are the expressions and developments of the conviction, that the soul is immortal, and will live and act after the body dies. It is true that in some cases this instinct

[1] Eccle. xii. 7.

may seem to be overpowered by dread or by arguments, but seldom, if ever, can it be eradicated.

With the certainty of immortality has always been associated the conviction that disembodied souls recognize each other. Indeed these two thoughts go together. They are taught by the same natural instinct, they necessarily involve each other, and mutually depend upon the permanent characteristics of the soul. The ancient poets and soothsayers, in every description of the spirit world, called the souls by their earthly names and represented them as associating and co-operating, as communicating information and feeling, as they had done in this world. They spoke indeed of the waters of Lethe, but only because in some cases forgetfulness was deemed necessary. The Egyptians and Hindoos, in maintaining their doctrine of the transmigration of souls, were forced to account in some way for the unnatural inability to recall the experiences in former states and bodies.

There are some forms of Christian beliefs which involve the denial of the recognition of souls. Certain views of the final judgment require the assumption that between death and the last day all are in an undetermined state, asleep—unconscious of their own existence and the presence of others. Many regard the soul as so dependent upon the bodily organs that it can perceive neither material nor spiritual things. Such conclusions do violence to our natures and our instinctive aspirations, and ought not to be received, unless clearly taught in the Word of God. What the Scriptures teach on the subject we shall presently examine. But let us remember that those who believe in immortality, naturally and very generally hold that after the death of the body we shall possess and exercise, at least, the same mental and spiritual faculties that we do now, that we shall know each other, and shall communicate and co-operate. This conviction is so strong as almost to be an assurance. Indeed it is seldom formally denied.

II.

OBJECTIONS EXAMINED.

BEFORE considering the grounds for this general conviction, it may be well to examine some of the objections which have been urged against this precious doctrine.

I. THE DEPENDENCE OF THE SOUL UPON THE BODY. It is asserted that so close is the union, and so absolute the dependence, that the one can do nothing without the other. No information can reach the soul save through the bodily organs, and by these alone can there be any expression of feeling and will. This statement must be received with some reservation. For while God usually reveals His will through the reading and hearing of His word, He is by no means thus restricted. In inspiration He has often imparted truth by vision and audible voice, but also not unfrequently has operated directly upon the spirits of the prophets. The method may not be understood, but men "spake as they were moved by the Holy Ghost,"[1] and "searched what or what manner of time the Spirit of Christ which was in them did signify."[2] In regeneration and sanctification, outward means are used, but the Spirit also works immediately, producing the new birth and transformation after the image of God. In temptation, an unseen and spiritual contest is carried on, the angels minister and strengthen, and devils blind and harden the heart and strive to "deceive the very elect."

Nevertheless there is a real dependence

[1] II Pet. i. 21.   [2] I Pet. i. 11

upon the body. The five senses are the appointed channels of communication with external objects. If these be one by one destroyed, we are gradually shut in, and at last are unable to perceive or express anything. But it must be remembered that the faculties of perception still remain after the organs are destroyed. A prisoner in a dungeon would possess sight and hearing, even if no ray of light nor wave of sound could reach him. Or if through some opening he could catch a glimpse of the outer world, his power of vision would not be destroyed if that loophole were again closed. Prison doors have been opened and the solitary one has been brought forth to wider vision and perfect liberty. Through the little orifice of the eye we can see something, but when this prison house of flesh shall be destroyed we shall go forth to clear light and perfect vision. "Now we see through a glass darkly, but then face to face."[1] One born deaf, nevertheless possesses the faculty of hearing. If by an operation the obstructions are removed and sounds reach the auditory nerve, the unknown sense awakens with delight. Could the sensitive soul be set free from its present encasement, it would drink in the harmony by which it would be surrounded. Moses, on the mount of transfiguration, needed not the organs of his body, which was still " buried in the land of Moab."[2] The souls under the altar and the redeemed from the earth, while waiting for the resurrection, can hear and join the praises which surround the throne, and can speak, " Oh Lord how long?" and receive the answer "that they should rest yet for a little season."[3]

II. THE CHARACTER OF THE JUDGMENT. Some assert that the souls both of the right-

[1] I Cor. xiii. 12. [2] Deut. xxxiv. 6. [3] Rev. vi. 10, 11.

eous and of the wicked must be in a state of unconsciousness, and are described as "asleep" until the trial at the last day, when they are to be judged of the deeds done in the body, and their everlasting reward or punishment is to be determined. And that this final judgment would be unmeaning, if at death they enter into blessedness or misery.

The force of this objection lies in a misinterpretation of Scripture, and a wrong view of the character of the judgment. The word "asleep" is applied to the dead, and in the New Testament only to the righteous dead; and evidently in every passage refers to the state of the body and not to that of the soul. "Many that sleep in the dust of the earth shall awake."[1] "I go that I may awake him [Lazarus] out of sleep."[2] "We shall not all sleep, but we shall all be changed."[3] Even "the souls un-

[1] Dan. xii. 2. [2] John xi. 11. [3] I Cor. xv. 51.

der the altar," while "resting yet a little season,"¹ make their petitions, receive their white robes and are told to wait for their fellow-servants. It was not to unconsciousness that our Lord welcomed the dying thief —" To-day shalt thou be with me in Paradise."²

The object of the final judgment is not to determine, as in an earthly court, whether we be guilty or not guilty, what degrees of reward or punishment each should receive, nor whether we be in Christ or out of Christ. To a certain degree even we, and while we are still in the flesh, are assured of proper answers to these questions. And to God, the Judge, all things are known from the beginning. "He needed not that any should testify of man, for He knew what was in man."³ He knows His own sheep, "whom the Father

---

¹ Rev. vi. 11.   ² Luke xxiii. 43.   ³ John ii. 25.

hath given."[1] The angels "that are sent forth to minister to them who shall be the heirs of salvation"[2] can distinguish between "the sheep and the goats."[3] The judgment is the grand exhibition of the glory of Christ, in which He will publicly pronounce sentence upon each, vindicate all His dealings with men and devils, exhibit the universality of His absolute and undisputed dominion over all, and before His Father and the holy angels openly acknowledge and acquit His redeemed and banish His enemies. (See "Confession of Faith," chap. 32; "Shorter Catechism, q. 38, and all that the Scriptures say of the judgment, as in Matthew xxv: and in II Thessalonians i.) To attain these objects, He "shall bring every work into judgment, with every secret, thing, whether it be good or whether it be evil."[4]

[1] John x. 27, 29.
[2] Heb. i. 14.
[3] Matt. xiii. 49; xxv. 32.
[4] Eccle. xii. 14.

At the resurrection we shall indeed "lift up our heads, for our redemption draweth nigh."[1] "We are waiting for the adoption, to wit, the redemption, of our bodies."[2] We shall then "enter into the joy of our Lord,"[3] "inherit the kingdom prepared for us from the foundation of the world."[4] But this does not necessitate the unnatural and unscriptural assumption that until the last great day we must remain in silent dormitories, unconscious of self or others, and insensible to happiness or misery.

III. THE CHARACTER OF HEAVEN. The Scriptures teach that "to be absent from the body is to be present with the Lord."[5] And they describe the bliss of heaven as consisting in beholding the face of Christ, admiring His glory and praising His infinite grace. It is

[1] Luke xxi. 28. [2] Rom. viii. 23. [3] Matt. xxv. 23.
[4] Matt. xxv. 34. [5] II Cor. v. 8.

said, however, that so ecstatic will be this vision, that the whole soul will be absorbed in the contemplation and in the expression of delight. That the consciousness of other objects, however beautiful or loved, would be distracting and would destroy perfect enjoyment.

This is an unauthorized assumption. It may be true, because of present infirmity, that when we come suddenly upon a grand view of beauty or power—as on some mountain top or near a mighty cataract—we are overwhelmed with wonder and gaze with delight, forgetful of everything else. We are alone, though multitudes may stand with us. Speech is an interruption not to be permitted. But as we begin to appreciate the grandeur, our natures demand expression and sympathy. We must utter God's praise and call on rocks and trees and men to join us in our song. Our joy cannot otherwise be complete. Adam found not, in the garden of Eden, a paradise until Eve was given to join in his worship. Heaven would not be heaven if each soul were isolated in solitary awe. Indeed we cannot see Christ alone. "He that seeth me, seeth My Father also"[1]—not merely because "He is in the Father and the Father in Him," but also because the Father and the Son are always together. "If a man love me, he will keep my words, and my Father will love him, and we will come unto him and make our abode with him."[2] At conversion we are led by the Holy Ghost to the Son, who presents us to the Father. The three persons cannot be dissociated. If we receive or reject one, we necessarily receive or reject the others. If we hold communion with the Son, we do so with the Father and Spirit. When "we see Christ as He is,"[3] we shall also see the Father

[1] John xii. 45; xiv. 9.   [2] John xiv. 23.   [3] John iii. 2

face to face, and admiringly worship the three persons of the Godhead. The glory will be overpowering, we may even "fall at His feet as dead men,"[1] until He touches us, and speaks to us, and calls forth our expressions of adoration. When Joseph made himself known to his brethren, they "could not answer him," but he drew them near, talked a good while, kissed them and wept upon them, "after that they talked with him" and were filled with real joy.[2]

This Triune God is never alone. Whenever manifested, He is surrounded by adoring beings. At the creation all the angels "shouted for joy."[3] The cherubim indicated His presence at the gates of Eden, and on the mercy seat. Whenever He revealed Himself to the patriarchs, the people from Sinai, or to the prophets, He was accompa-

[1] Rev. i. 17.   [2] Gen. xlv. 3-15.   [3] Job xxxviii. 7.

nied by angels. When Jesus was seen in His glory in the incarnation, in the transfiguration, in the atonement, in the resurrection and ascension, He was surrounded by ministering spirits, and when He shall come a second time, it shall be with the innumerable hosts of God.[1] Buddha may be represented as absorbed in silent self-contemplation, but our God is ever associated with His creatures, thinking upon them and receiving their adoration. When we, like John on Patmos, see the Lamb in the midst of the throne, we shall behold the four living creatures and the four and twenty elders and the innumerable company of saints and angels. We cannot therefore see God without beholding also the hosts of heaven, hearing their adoration and being drawn into their communion.

The nature of God is expressed in His

[1] Matt. xxv. 31.

works and more clearly revealed in His commandments. These are summed up in two tables which cannot be separated. Love to God involves love to men. "If a man say, I love God, and hateth his brother, he is a liar; for he that loveth not his brother, whom he hath seen, how can he love God, whom he hath not seen?"[1] This is true, however love is manifested. "If thou bring thy gift to the altar, and there rememberest that thy brother hath aught against thee; leave there thy gift before the altar and go thy way, first be reconciled to thy brother and then come and offer thy gift."[2] Worship in service must be unto the Lord and in co-operation with others. No member can say to others, "I have no need of you."[3] Full communion with the Lord is only possible in communion with His people. This necessity does not arise from our

[1] I John iv. 20.   [2] Matt. v. 23, 24.   [3] I Cor. xii. 21.

present condition, but from the character of God as revealed in His law. The more we admire and adore God, the more must we admire Him "in all them that believe,"[1] and join in their adoration. "His delights are in the sons of men,"[2] and they who are transformed into His image, in heaven as on earth, love Him with all the heart, and their neighbor as themselves. Communion of saints is a part of the joy of heaven and is essential to the worship of Christ. When the three disciples "were eye witnesses of His majesty"[3] in the holy mount, they saw also Moses and Elias, although "His face did shine as the sun, and His raiment was white as the light."[4] When the eleven beheld Him ascend to His glory at the right hand of the Father—they saw also the angels which stood by them.[5] And when

[1] II Thes. i. 10. [2] Prov. viii. 31. [3] II Peter i. 16.
[4] Matt. xvii. 2, 3. [5] Acts i. 10, 11.

He comes again every eye shall see Him and the holy angels with Him.[1]

IV. OUR OWN NATURES. God has made us of one blood, and has set us in families. We are bone of bone and flesh of flesh. Character, mental and spiritual peculiarities, are transmitted from parent to child, and distinguish and bind together families in unions most close and lasting. It is the impulse of nature and the highest teaching of religion, "to love one another," "to lay down our lives for the brethren,"[2] and to endure any self-sacrifice for the safety and happiness of our own. It is said that with such natures, to us heaven would be an impossibility if recognition were permitted. For how could a parent be happy, if among the redeemed he would miss the child over whom he had always yearned with heart desire and prayer that he might be saved.

[1] Rev. i. 7.   [2] I John iii. 16.

This objection is a serious one, and may not be fully answered at present. But inability to recognize would only increase the difficulty and the anguish, leav'ng us forever uncertain as to the destiny of each and all whom we have loved, and causing us to begin eternity as absolute strangers. Such a thought is in violation of every instinct of our nature. It were better to believe that God could in some way comfort us concerning the absence of a few, than to conclude it necessary that He should conceal from us His most righteous decisions in regard to all.

The Scriptures teach that our condition after death is the continuation, as well as the result, of our life on earth and of God's dealings with us. Love for each other and the communion of saints will be perfected there, not destroyed. It is divine comfort, as well as human hope, which, with David, says as each dear one leaves us—"I shall go to him, but he shall not return to me."[1] "They shall receive us into everlasting habitations."[2] It were better to hold fast this assurance, imparted alike by instinct and inspiration, even were we unable to conceive how the promised happiness can be secured. Yet we admire the patriot who, from love of country, will not know son or daughter who has proved a traitor to fatherland. We do not blame the apostles because, through love to Christ, they made no lamentation at the death of Judas, who had betrayed their Master with a kiss. And when we shall understand the real character of sin, and the guilt of trampling under foot the Son of God, we will hate father and mother, son and daughter, who are the determined enemies of our Lord and Saviour. We cannot indeed bear the thought now, because

[1] II Sam. xii. 23.   [2] Luke xvi. 9.

their probation is not ended, and we are prompted by our own natures, by the example of Christ, and by the impulse of the Holy Ghost, to yearn over them and to labor for their salvation. But when infinite love says "It is enough—" "they be joined to their idols"—"let them alone"[1]—we will see the justice and holiness of God; and as we love Him, we can not love them who hate God and are under His curse. We will be in Christ, and regard all things as related to Him. We will love them who love Christ, but we will have no fellowship with nor interest in those who hate Him.

Other objections have been urged. But they all arise from ignorance, want of experience, or from inferences drawn from what we suppose to be truth, or which seem necessary to remove certain difficulties. They

[1] Hosea iv. 17.

are overcome by a clearer knowledge of what has been revealed in the Scriptures, and by faith that Christ can secure perfect happiness to His saints in communion with Him and each other.

III.

TEACHING OF SCRIPTURES.

THE only reliable information concerning the state of the soul after death is to be found in the Word of God. The instruction thus given is far more definite than is generally supposed. Much is presented by direct statement, and by comparison and contrast with what we have seen and experienced. And much is assumed as undeniably true and not needing proof or illustration. As the being of God is taken for granted, as an undeniable fact, so is the permanency of the essential characteristics of our nature. We must always possess intelligence, affections, a conscience, a self-determining will, and we will ever exercise these faculties towards God and each other. Every passage presumes that we will be hereafter, as now, reverential and social beings—loving God and one another. This necessarily includes recognition, communion with Christ, His angels and His redeemed.

Those passages, therefore, are pertinent to this question, which ascribe distinguishing names to angels and to devils, and describe them as conversing, co-operating or contending with each other and with the souls in heaven or hell, and with men in the flesh. It is assumed that angels, though spirits, can recognize each other—when we are told of their creation, their union as the hosts of God, their organization as principalities and powers in high places, their history, some keeping their first estate and others sinning and being cast out of heaven, reserved unto judgment,[1] their employment in the mysteries of providence and redemption,[2] and their connection with material things and beings, severally appointed over nations,[3] ministering to saints,[4] guarding the body of Moses[5]—filling the air,[6] covering the hills,[7] entering Eden,[8] "going to and fro in the earth, and walking up and down in it,"[9] appearing unto men, conversing with them, tempting them, possessing their bodies, or delivering them from prison.[10]

If spirits can thus fellowship, and can have dealings with men, recognition of souls is not an impossibility, but a necessity. If Michael can dispute with the devil, Abraham, Isaac, and Jacob can converse. If Gabriel could tell Mary that she should conceive a

[1] Jude, 6. [2] Matt. iv. 6. [3] Dan. x. 13-21. [4] Heb. i. 14.
[5] Jude, 9. [6] Eph. ii. 2. [7] II Kings vi. 17. [8] Gen. iii. 1.
[9] Job ii. 2. [10] Acts xii. 7.

Son,[1] farther communications did not become impossible when the virgin mother, also as a spirit, "stood before God." And the angel which showed John the New Jerusalem from the Isle of Patmos, showed him great things when he entered with him into this spiritual city.

It may be said, that, whenever spirits held communications with men, they assumed some corporeal form, and that this is necessary. But the thought now urged is, that spirits can see and converse with spirits, and angels with angels, and therefore souls with souls. Nor is it true that when the immaterial hold intercourse with the material, it must have fleshly organs. Abraham is not described as seeing the angel which called to him out of heaven. Saul's companions heard a voice, but saw no one. Satan did appear to Eve as a serpent.

[1] Luke i. 31.

Angels to the patriarchs as travellers, and to the Marys as young men, to remove fear and gain attention without distraction. It is our infirmities, and not our spirits' necessities, which make visible forms expedient. Our bodily eyes cannot discern spiritual things, else we could see at all times, as the servant of Elisha did when his eyes were opened, " the mountains full of horses and chariots of fire round about God's people,"[1] " ministering to them who shall be the heirs of salvation."[2] Even Moses had to conceal his face with a veil when on Sinai his skin caught some of the spiritual glory ;[3] and Christ humbled Himself as the Man of Sorrow that He might be the friend of sinners. When the three disciples saw His glory in the mount—" They were sore afraid," as were the shepherds, who heard the angels' song near Bethlehem. It is

[1] II Kings vi. 17.   [2] Heb. i. 14.   [3] Ex. xxxiv. 35.

expedient for us, not necessary for the spirits, that they appear as men, and although we do not perceive them, "in their hands they bear us up, lest at any time we dash our foot against a stone." [1]

In the Old Testament death is often described thus—"Thou shalt go to thy fathers." [2] "He was gathered to his people," [3] or "to his fathers." [4] That these expressions do not refer to the burial of the body is evident, because they are used only in regard to the righteous dead, and have in all cases an evident connection with the covenant made with Abraham and his seed; and because they sometimes describe the departure of those who were not buried in family sepulchres, as Abraham, Moses, and David. They can refer only to the promise and hope

[1] Matt. iv. 6.   [2] Gen. xv. 15.
[3] Num. xx. 24.   [4] Acts. xiii. 36.

of meeting the souls of those who had died in faith—" so great a cloud of witnesses,"[1] who have entered the rest and inherited the promises. " The God of Abraham, and the God of Isaac, and the God of Jacob," is " not the God of the dead but of the living."[2]

This expectation of again seeing those who have died is frequently expressed, as by David concerning his child, " I shall go to him."[3] It is promised by Christ. " Ye shall see Abraham, and Isaac, and Jacob, and all the prophets in the kingdom of God." " And they shall come from the east, and from the west, and from the north, and from the south, and shall sit down in the Kingdom of God."[4] " That ye may eat and drink at My table."[5] " Blessed are they which are called unto the

---

[1] Heb. xii. 1. [2] Matt. xxii. 32. [3] II Sam. xii. 23.
[4] Luke xiii. 28, 29. [5] Luke xxii. 30.

marriage supper of the Lamb."[1] It is either directly asserted or pre-supposed in every passage that refers to heaven, and especially in all those parables which represent that place as a kingdom, a house with servants, a great supper, a marriage feast, a city, a temple with worshippers. For these imply and necessitate association and communion. Those who are shut out are described as remembering their individual and collective hypocritical treatment of Christ, and as speaking for one another as well as personally. "Lord, have we not prophesied in Thy name, and in Thy name have cast out devils, and in Thy name have done many wonderful works?"[2]

We have also several cases narrated of recognition. Samuel appeared to Saul.[3] It is acknowledged that there are difficulties of

[1] Rev. xix. 9.   [2] Matt. vii. 22.   [3] I Sam. xxviii. 7-20.

interpretation to be met in this passage, as to the power of the witch of Endor, by what means Samuel was recalled, whether the woman expected his appearance or was terrified at what God accomplished, and whether Saul himself beheld the spiritual form. But there is no difficulty as to the important facts. Samuel had died. The Lord had refused to communicate, through the ordinary means of grace, with the rebellious king, who desired an interview with the dead prophet. Samuel appeared, "and Saul perceived that it was Samuel, and he stooped his face to the ground and bowed himself." The seer spake to the king, who answered, "I have called thee that thou mayest make known unto me what I shall do." And Samuel in the name of the Lord reproved him for his sin and pronounced upon him the swift judgment of God. This is stated as a real interview, between parties formerly associated and now brought together again. They are described as conversing in the same way as when Samuel was in the flesh. Saul asks for divine guidance, and Samuel utters true prophecy, which is immediately, yet strangely, fulfilled.

On the Mount of Transfiguration, two men appeared with Christ in His glory.[1] This is a marvellous scene, and made a deep impression upon Peter, James and John. So far as they were concerned, it was designed to sustain their faith during the dark hours, so near, of the crucifixion and burial of their Lord. It throws much light on the question now before us. The three glorified ones are—Christ, a man in the flesh; Moses, a disembodied soul; and Elias, who had been caught up into heaven, whose body had become spiritual and glorified. In them we see the three stages of

[1] Luke ix. 28-36.

man's existence. But in these states they recognize each other and talk concerning "the decease which should be accomplished at Jerusalem." Their different conditions offer no bar to their intercourse, no explanation is needed of their knowledge of each other nor of their methods of communication. All is most natural and easy. It is to be noticed further that in their life-time they were separated by ages. They lived in the three great epochs of the history of the Church. They, as the miracle workers, represent the different dispensations which they severally introduced, of the law, of reformation, and grace. In this scene they typify and demonstrate the communion of saints of all ages, whether in the flesh, in the spirit, or in glorified bodies; on earth, in heaven, and through eternity. It is not merely a prophecy of future union and association, but a realization of that unseen conference, which is carried on by the glorified, concerning what is doing on earth. The awakening disciples are amazed, but seeing and hearing the men, they say, "Master, it is good for us to be here, and let us make three tabernacles, one for Thee, one for Moses, and one for Elias." We need not now inquire how they know these ancient prophets. It is clear that they did know them, called them by name and desired to make the delightful interview more lasting, and to derive further instruction from their strange conversation.

In the parable of the rich man and Lazarus [1] we have another revelation. It seems certain that most, if not all, the parables of Christ were taken from real life, and describe persons and facts known to His hearers. This one has special indications of being actual his-

[1] Luke xvi. 19-31.

tory. "There was a certain rich man, which was clothed in purple and fine linen, and fared sumptuously every day. And there was a certain beggar named Lazarus, which was laid at his gate, full of sores." There can be no doubt, however, that in closing the sermon recorded in Luke xv. and xvi., Christ intended in this parable to lift the veil which now hides the unseen world, and permit us to trace the after history of the two great classes of men which He had been describing. "And it came to pass that the beggar died, and was carried by the angels into Abraham's bosom." These spirits continue visibly the ministration which they, unseen, have long carried on. However the expression "Abraham's bosom" may be interpreted, it certainly implies that the newly transported soul knew into whose bosom he was placed, and by whom he was comforted. He knew Abraham, the patriarch, to whom the rest had been promised, or the gathered seed of Abraham, who were enjoying with him and each other the covenanted inheritance. It is worth while to notice that the highest joy of heaven, seeing God, is not here referred to, except in very dim figure. The view presented is that of rest from the trials of earth, and the comfort in the society of Abraham and his seed which must therefore form an essential element of bliss. The restful communion of Lazarus with these most illustrious saints is strongly contrasted with his wretched lowliness as a beggar outside the gate of the rich man. This association cannot be interrupted by a call, however importunately made, even for an act of mercy to a suffering soul, nor yet for a testimony to those who will not hear the ordinary means of grace, "Moses and the prophets."

"The rich man also died, and was buried;

and in hell he lifted up his eyes, being in torments, and seeth Abraham afar off, and Lazarus in his bosom. And he cried and said, Father Abraham, have mercy on me and send Lazarus." This is a very vivid picture of the condition of the wicked after death, and contains some details not seen so clearly elsewhere—as the suddenness and severity of the torment, the denial of the least alleviation, the impossibility of passing to or fro over the great gulf fixed between heaven and hell. Our present purpose, however, confines our attention to the fact that the wicked soul is essentially the same as before death. He remembers his former life, its associations are still realities, though past. Human ties still bind him to his brethren, not merely as intimacies which can not be forgotten, but as associations soon to be renewed. He, for the first time, perhaps, prays for their conversion, either because of interest in them, "lest they also come into this place of torment," or from fear of increased anguish in witnessing their sufferings or in enduring their revenge. His twice repeated prayer and earnest argument are prompted by anticipated recognition. He is still the same man. He perceives Lazarus. He does not doubt his identity. He calls him unhesitatingly by name, and notwithstanding the new society and surroundings in Abraham's bosom, he regards him, until informed to the contrary, as one to be ordered about, and to minister to him. "Send Lazarus, that he may dip the tip of his finger in water and cool my tongue."

How he recognized Abraham, or those represented in him, we need not now inquire. But it is stated that, however far off, he did see Abraham and Lazarus. Whether with them there were few or many, he distinguished these two, and at once, without doubt, called them by name—"Father Abraham, have mercy on me, and send Lazarus." The conversation, as narrated in eight verses, is most free and emphatic, and demonstrates the impossibility of post-mortem repentance, the inefficacy of prayer from hell, the permanency of human affections, the sufficiency of the means of grace, the undisturbed rest of the righteous and the continued misery of the wicked. But the mere fact of this long conversation proves that souls, immediately after death, do recognize each other and commune, and that this recognition greatly increases the enjoyment of the righteous and the sufferings of the wicked.

It may be said that this is an imaginary conversation, introduced to enforce the previous discourse. But we must remember that the preacher is Christ, that He could not present an imaginary scene contrary to facts; that He could not enforce His doctrine by false suppositions, and misrepresentations, of eternal realities. He here describes the state of the soul after death. Recognition is not an unimportant accident in the scene. It is an essential fact. Everything depends upon it—the happiness of the redeemed, the increased misery of the lost, the conversation between Abraham and Dives, the desired communication with the living, and the anticipated association in torments. All this is emphasized by the fact that this is the only parable which Christ has given concerning the soul immediately after death. There is nothing to modify the impression which He has here given, that recognition is an essential element of the future condition of the saved and of the lost.

On the cross, Christ said to the dying thief,

"To-day shalt thou be with me in Paradise."[1] It is absurd to imagine that this gracious promise means that when their souls should leave their suffering bodies, they would become unconscious of each other's presence. The thief prayed to be "remembered in His Kingdom," and Christ assured him of association that day with Him in glory.

The promise "I will come again and receive you unto myself, that where I am, there ye may be also,"[2] has long ago been fulfilled. And as the last of the twelve entered His presence, they perceived that "not one of them was lost but the son of perdition; that the Scripture might be fulfilled."[3] Stephen, while being martyred, "saw the heavens opened, and the Son of man standing on the right hand of God"[4] to welcome him. He did

[1] Luke xxiii. 43.
[2] John xiv. 3.
[3] John xvii. 12.
[4] Acts vii. 56.

not pass into unconsciousness, nor is he isolated from the many who like him have been "slain for the testimony of Jesus."[1] Paul recognized the souls given as "the seals of his ministry"[2] and "the crown of his rejoicing."[3] "They have received him into everlasting habitations."[4] Indeed every allusion in Scripture to the state of the soul after death, and especially the whole book of Revelation, assumes and declares that recognition is a fact, and is essential to the enjoyment of the redeemed in heaven.

This Scripture proof is, as we have seen, in accord with our instincts and natural longing. It seems also to explain the experience of not a few who, as they were departing, declared that they saw and heard what others could

[1] Rev. vi. 9.
[2] I Cor. ix. 2.
[3] I Thes. ii. 19.
[4] Luke xvi. 9.

not discern. They spoke, as did Stephen, of glorious visions of Christ, of the sight of faces and forms for years numbered with the dead. They smiled in glad recognition, and departed with long cherished names upon their lips.

IV.

IN THE IMAGE OF GOD.

A VERY important part of the teaching of Scripture on this subject is the revelation of the nature of God. For God said, "Let us make man in our image, after our likeness." "So God created man in His own image, in the image of God created He him."[1] We cannot therefore understand what we are, or what is to be our destiny, until we are taught something of the nature of God. Because of this resemblance, we are authorized to believe that whatever is essential to us must be ascribed, freed from all imperfec-

[1] Gen. i. 26, 27.

tions, also unto the Lord. Because we have certain attributes in a finite degree, we know that " God is a spirit, infinite, eternal and unchangeable in His being, wisdom, power, holiness, justice, goodness and truth." Indeed the attributes we do not possess cannot be conceived by us, nor ascribed to God. But it is also true, that in so far as God reveals to us the mysteries of His nature, we learn what we are and what we shall be, when developed in His image, from glory unto glory.

As we enter upon this study we are met at once with a wonderful doctrine, which we cannot comprehend, but which is clearly revealed. In the unity of the Godhead there are three persons. Many regard this as a mere mystery, to be received because revealed, to be regarded with awe as pertaining to the divine existence and operations, but which can have no practical application to us. Nevertheless, it has been revealed, and is designed to teach us to adore and serve the triune God. This doctrine has a very important bearing upon the recognition of souls. For although God is infinite, eternal, and unchangeable, absolutely independent of all external objects, needing not the service nor adoration of any creature, self-centered, and with no object save His own glory, yet in the very constitution of the divine nature there is this essential element of sociability. From all eternity, the Father, the Son, and the Holy Ghost were, and these three are one God. The following words are recorded as the utterance of one of the persons of the Godhead—it may be questioned whether the Son or the Holy Ghost is the speaker—"The Lord possessed me in the beginning of His way, before His works of old. I was set up from everlasting, from the beginning, or ever the earth was. .... When He prepared the heavens, I was there; when He set a compass upon the face of the depth; when He established the clouds above; when He strengthened the fountains of the deep; when He gave the sea His decree . . . when He appointed the foundations of the earth, then I was by Him, as one brought up with Him: and I was daily His delight, rejoicing always before Him."[1] And Christ prays, "O Father, glorify Thou Me with thine own self, with the glory which I had with Thee before the world was."[2] There ever have been three persons in the Godhead. All we know of the one God is the unfolding of the relationships of the Father, Son, and Holy Ghost. Their attributes are held in common, and are exercised upon each other. There is

---

[1] Prov. viii. 22-30. [2] John xvii. 5.

but one love of God, yet the Father loves the Son, the Son loves the Father and sends the Spirit, and the Spirit proceeds from the Father and the Son. We are told that in eternity were counsel, communication, plan, decrees, and covenant, between these three persons. In all the divine purpose there is agreement. In every act, all co-operate. "The Son can do nothing of Himself, but whatsoever He seeth the Father do; for what things soever He doeth, these also doeth the Son likewise."[1] And the "Spirit shall not speak of Himself, but whatsoever He shall hear, that shall He speak. . . . He shall glorify Me, for He shall receive of mine and shall shew it unto you."[2] Creation, Providence, and Redemption are therefore ascribed alike to the Father, Son, and Holy Ghost, because all are constantly active

[1] John v. 19.   [2] John xvi. 13, 14.

therein. What the Father does, He does by the Son and through the Holy Ghost. And in our reception of grace, we can approach only as drawn by the Spirit to Christ, and by Him we come to the Father. In the very nature of God, therefore, there is mutual recognition, with consultation and co-operation.

Whatever motive prompted God to create must be found in Himself. His full purpose, of course, we cannot comprehend, but it is evident that this social element of His nature found expression when He filled all space with His works, and when He formed the angels, the innumerable hosts of heaven, to surround His throne, to worship and serve Him. He delights in their companionship, seeks their sympathy, and performs His most divine works through their agency. As He creates, they shout for joy. His providence is administered through their instrumentality. They are the medium by which the law is given, they announce the incarnation, they strengthen Him in temptation and in agony, they guard His body, declare His resurrection, welcome Him back to glory, and when He shall sit in judgment they will attend Him and execute His decrees.

"His delight in the sons of men"[1] is also to be noticed—communing with them in the garden, pitying them at the fall, unwilling that they should perish, appearing often personally to them, taking up His abode even with the rebellious race, delighting to answer their prayers, manifesting Himself even to two or three met in His name, rejoicing over every lost one recovered, carrying their names on His heart and hands. This may seem incredible, "for what is man that Thou

[1] Prov. viii. 31.

takest knowledge of him ? or the son of man, that Thou makest account of him ?"[1] It is, nevertheless, a fact, and this wonderful love is not excited by man's ability or worthiness, but is prompted by the very nature of God.

Perhaps the most marvellous manifestation of this element of His nature is to be found in the manner in which He carries on His great work of redemption, the establishing His kingdom on earth. There was plausible reason and force in the Devil's three-fold temptation of Christ, that, without the delay and sufferings of centuries, He should set up His kingdom immediately, by direct divine power, or by the agency of angels, or by compromise.[2] But the divine wisdom had planned that it should be by the atonement of the Son of God and the foolishness of preaching. Men " have fellowship in His

[1] Ps. cxliv. 3.   [2] Matt. iv. 3-10

sufferings,"[1] and are called "to fill up that which is behind of the afflictions of Christ."[2] In the application of salvation, He confines His operations to the voluntary activity of His people, as they "preach the gospel to every creature."[3] Without them He does nothing. They are co-laborers with Christ, fellow-sufferers and joint heirs. They "bring. many sons unto glory."[4] We often dwell upon this, as the high privilege and glory of Christians, and their responsibility to be zealous and diligent even to the end. But if we seek the motive for this method of grace, we must find it in the nature of God. He delights in communication, fellowship, co-operation, and joint participation of His love, work, throne, and glory.

If this sociability be an essential character-

[1] Phil. iii. 10. [2] Col. i. 24.
[3] Mark xvi. 15. [4] Heb. ii. 10, 11.

istic of the divine nature, when He made man after His image and likeness, He did not merely give him powers to perceive that there is a God, to hear His word, and to adore Him, but He constituted him to be like God, craving sympathy and communion. Man needed the fellowship vouchsafed in the cool of the day in Eden, but, blessed as these interviews were, Adam was finite and God infinite. Man was yet alone in his worship and could not be satisfied, and " God said it is not good that the man should be alone." [1] No mate could be found in lower forms of life. The helpmeet needed by man, in his unfallen state of perfection, was his equal, not superior nor inferior, but a co-worshipper of God. That this God-like social craving of his nature might be satisfied, " God made a woman and brought her unto the man." [1]

[1] Gen. ii. 18.   [2] Gen. ii. 23.

He has set men in families. He has ordained races, tribes, and nations. He gathers them as peoples, and binds all flesh together as of one blood, so that in every approach to God they must recognize the whole brotherhood of man. "Our Father which art in heaven."[1] No one can ask for any personal favor without thereby invoking temporal and spiritual blessings on others. No man liveth to himself, each is his neighbor's keeper. This is not the result of sin and the fall, but the characteristic of human nature made in the image of God. Sin tends to alienate men, and renders them "devoid of natural affections."[2] Grace restores the divine likeness, and brotherly love abounds. Moses even prayed, "Yet now, if Thou wilt forgive their sin; and if not, blot me, I pray Thee, out of the book which Thou hast written."[3] And

[1] Matt. vi. 9.   [2] Rom. i. 31.   [3] Ex. xxxii. 32.

Paul says, "I could wish that myself were accursed from Christ for my brethren, my kinsmen according to the flesh."[1] When we shall be perfect as He is perfect, awake in His likeness, love will be the grace which shall abide, as the greatest and most essential. The fellowship into which Jesus drew the twelve was not merely personal attachment to Him, but also most intimate association with each other—to labor and suffer together, to share the twelve thrones, and to be the united foundations of the New Jerusalem. "He loved Martha, her sister, and Lazarus,"[2] and sanctified their love, which death, the grave and the resurrection, would only render more holy and enduring. These sanctified affections and intimacies bring us into close conformity with Him who "loved His own which were in the world, and loved

[1] Rom. ix. 3.   [2] John xi. 5.

them unto the end,"[1] and prayed that "they might be with Him where He is, and behold His glory."[2] And when we shall gather in the mansions which He has prepared for us in the Father's house, we shall enjoy the communion of all saints, but we shall take special delight in our own by nature, and in those whom on earth we have loved in the Lord.

[1] John xiii. 1.   [2] John xvii. 24.

V.

METHODS OF RECOGNITION.

WE must now consider how we shall recognize each other. The fact of recognition is all important, and being clearly revealed is comforting and satisfactory. This would be so, even were the methods at present to us incomprehensible. Our faith and comfort, however, would be increased if we could perceive by what means we shall know each other. While there is no direct statement how this is to be accomplished, yet much is intimated and assumed as beyond question. We will doubtless possess new faculties and have enlarged capabilities for the reception of information, but these are beyond our present conception and cannot be considered. If, however, the fact of recognition is demonstrated as necessary because of the permanent characteristics and laws of our nature, it would seem more than probable that the means now used will be then also employed. According to the Scriptures, our life hereafter shall be a continuation, with a different environment, of our life on earth. At present, all external information comes to us through our five senses. We have already seen that these faculties do not depend upon the fleshly organs. Indeed, every description of souls after death attributes to them sight, hearing, and other sensations. We shall see God, His angels, and His redeemed; we shall hear their calls and join in their praise; we shall experience happiness, and the wicked shall suffer torments; we shall hold communion with each other as we now do on earth.

It is to be noticed that the more spiritualized become our perceptions, the more confident are we in our conclusions. Changes in outward appearance, caused by time, by suffering, or by assumed disguises, may perplex and deceive the eye, but parental instinct does not hesitate to discern the returning prodigal. Love and the knowledge of the inward peculiarities will set at defiance all outward appearances. We often doubt the testimony of our senses when, from the knowledge of the character and past life of a friend, we affirm that he is utterly incapable of certain conduct. Appearances may be against him, others may present unanswerable arguments and testimony, his own words may appear to have but one, and that a bad, construction, but, because of our personal knowledge of his principles, we do not doubt him, we are certain that all can be explained, and that he is innocent and honorable. Or, the facts may be undeniable, yet we do not distrust him. He may pass us as a stranger, we, though mortified and perplexed, are confident that he has some good reason for his unusual behavior. "Jonathan loved David as his own soul,"[1] and no representation of others, nor accusation of his own father, could induce him to suspect David of rebellion or discourtesy. The multitude in the temple knew that Jesus did hear and would reply, although He "stooped down and with His finger wrote on the ground."[2] The Syrophenician woman continued her prayer, "Have mercy on me, O Lord, thou Son of David; my daughter is grievously vexed with a devil!" "Lord help me!" although

[1] I Sam. xviii. 1.   [2] John viii. 6.

"He answered her not a word," but discouraged her by His converse with the disciples: "I am not sent but to the lost sheep of the house of Israel." "It is not meet to take the children's bread and cast it to dogs."[1] She was certain that He was very pitiful, that He healed every one brought to him and sent none empty away. Since our bodily faculties are imperfect, and what we perceive by them only indications of the real character and purposes, and these indications often very misleading, we cannot place entire reliance upon our bodily senses. We must be certain that we see and hear aright. We must use discrimination, be cautious, as in drawing conclusions, and be open to correction. Angels may appear as travellers; the devil, as an angel of light or as a serpent in the garden. During absence a

[1] Matt. xv. 21-28.

child attains manhood, and sorrow or joy transforms the countenance. We do not rely implicitly upon the testimony of our senses. We feel the need of mental and spiritual faculties, and though better satisfied with their conclusions, we are longing for some more reliable means of perception, and more direct and freer communication with others. This longing, we feel sure, will be realized. For both reason and revelation lead us to expect that when freed from the body our present faculties will be enlarged and perfected, and that new, more spiritual, powers will be granted to us. "Now we see through a glass darkly, but then face to face; now I know in part, but then shall I know even as also I am known."[1] We cannot imagine what additional means of perception and communication may be given to us, but

[1] I Cor. xiii. 12.

we know they will greatly aid our recognition of each other. At present we can consider only those now in use, but which will hereafter be freed from all their present imperfections.

VI.

RECOGNITION BY SPEECH.

ONE of the most significant names of God is "The Word." It implies His own infinite fulness and perfection, the existence of others who need information, His ability and readiness to impart truth, the clearness of His communications, and His great purpose in all things to reveal His own glory. The name also indicates the highest and fullest form of this revelation—by speech. All His works do indeed show forth His glory. The vast universe, with all created things, although pronounced "very good," is only a partial display of His glory.

In them can be clearly seen "His eternal power and Godhead."[1] But when by these things men "knew God, they glorified Him not as God, neither were thankful, but became vain in their imaginations and their foolish heart was darkened; professing themselves wise, they became fools, and changed the glory of the uncorruptible God into an image made like to corruptible man, and to birds, and four-footed beasts, and creeping things."[2] His providential dealings, although carried on according to an eternal plan, in infinite wisdom and without the least possible mistake, is incomprehensible even to the wisest and best of the saints. Abraham said in his perplexity, "Why go I thus childless?"[3] Jacob declared that "all these things are against me!"[4] and David "was envious

[1] Rom. i. 20.   [2] Rom. i. 21-23.
[3] Gen. xv. 2.   [4] Gen. xlii. 36.

of the foolish when he saw the prosperity of the wicked." "It was too painful for him until he went into the Sanctuary of God and understood their end."¹ The disciples often find that what God does "they know not now, although they shall know hereafter."² In the incarnation was manifested "all the fulness of the Godhead bodily."³ "The Word was made flesh and dwelt among us, and we beheld His glory, the glory as of the only begotten of the Father, full of grace and truth."⁴ But the facts of redemption, His birth, His life of perfect obedience, His shameful death, His resurrection and ascension, were not understood. They were a dark mystery, which the most wise and loving of His intimate friends could not solve. "Why hast Thou thus dealt with us?"⁵ "Lord, this

---

¹ Ps. lxxiii. 1–17.   ² John xiii. 7.   ³ Col. ii. 9.
⁴ John i. 14.   ⁵ Luke ii. 48.

shall not be unto Thee."[1] "We trusted that it had been He who should have redeemed Israel."[2] God was manifested in the flesh, salvation was accomplished; but it was the great mystery of godliness, the display of the harmonious operation of all the incomprehensible attributes of the divine nature. The meaning of this manifestation, the object and effect of this wonderful work, its connection with our characters and destiny—the gospel—could not be thus discerned. The highest and clearest form of revelation is by speech. External objects and acts may excite attention and illustrate, but we need "THE WORD," as God held communion with Adam, declared His covenant to Abraham, His law from Sinai, spake by the prophets, and taught on the mount, in the wilderness, in the temple, and in the upper room.

[1] Matt. xvi. 22.   [2] Luke xxiv. 21.

The angels worship God as they bow with veiled faces before His throne, and as they fly quickly to execute His will, but their most perfect worship is when in word and song they express their appreciation of His perfections and their admiration of His works and dealings. They unperceived minister to us, their encampment presents a barrier to our spiritual adversaries, but their freest intercourse is when they speak with human language to the patriarchs, Zacharias, Mary, the disciples and to John on Patmos; and when they cry one to another, or when they dispute with Satan, saying, "The Lord rebuke thee."[1]

The lower animals are not only guided by instinct, but have some means of communicating their apprehensions and desires. They inform, consult, plan and co-operate. Their

[1] Jude, 9.

means of communicating we have not detected, but it evidently corresponds with and takes the place of our speech.

Man is sometimes described as an animal with language. However imperfect may be this definition, it emphasizes a characteristic which raises man immeasurably above the brutes, and closely allies him with the highest created intelligences and with God Himself. A mother perhaps is never more happy than when her child begins to lisp the words which she teaches him. The deaf mutes were until lately in a condition of terrible isolation, and therefore of almost entire ignorance. The sign language has done much for them, but it is an imperfect and partial substitute for speech. Had it been good for Adam to be alone, he would not have needed language. But he was the head of a race. All his posterity was to be intimately connected with him, by nature and by covenant. All that was revealed to him, he must impart to them. His character, relations, conduct and destiny involved theirs. Men are gathered by God into nations and He sets them in families. They are all mutually dependent, they profit or suffer by each other's conduct. They by nature crave sympathy and fellowship. They must co-operate. Communication is an absolute necessity of man's very nature. Solitary confinement, exile, banishment, and non-intercourse are among the heaviest penalties which can be inflicted. Speech is the divinely appointed and only satisfactory means of communication. Eden would not have been a paradise to our first parents without communion with God and converse with each other. The confusion of tongues was a curse for sin, which separated and scattered mankind.[1] The gift of tongues was a blessing for the regathering of the nations and teaching of Christ's gospel to every creature.[2]

The application of all this to the state of the soul after death is very evident. We have seen that communication, and that by speech, is not an accident necessitated by our present environment, but a permanent ordinance to meet an essential characteristic of our nature and our unending relations to God, to angels and to each other. Our removal from earth to heaven will no more render speech unnecessary or improper than our change of residence from New York to Philadelphia. It is to be noticed that we by speech hold no communion with the earthly, the brutes that perish, but only with those whose stay here is limited, and whose real life is in eternity. The subjects, too, of our

[1] Gen. xi. 7.   [2] Acts ii. 1-11.

converse are not material things. Of course these are referred to. There are those who are always saying, "What shall we eat? What shall we drink, and wherewithal shall we be clothed?"[1] But these are debasing their natures and misusing their powers. We have to do with material things, which were designed to be means for the acquisition of knowledge, the excitement to thought and development of emotions. Speech is not only adapted to set forth intellectual and spiritual things, but these are its most appropriate themes. In proportion as we attain to real manhood, our converse is rather of unseen realities, the conclusions of intellectual activity and meditation, the wealth of developed affections, the fullest sympathy with man and glowing adoration of God. All this

---

[1] Matt. vi. 31.

in the Christian is a spiritual development, and a preparation for heaven.

The ordinary objection that in heaven we will not have vocal and auditory organs, or a medium for vibrations, has already been answered. Every essential characteristic of our natures will there find its employment and satisfaction. The imperfection of human language will be rectified and free communication with God, the redeemed and the angels secured. It is therefore with no surprise that we read that heaven is vocal with praise, every tongue joining in the worship, and that communion of saints and with God constitutes the nature and the bliss of heaven. We cannot now inquire into the meaning of the passage, "And when he had opened the seventh seal, there was silence in heaven about the space of half an hour,"[1] whether this refers to a ce-

[1] Rev. viii. 1.

lestial or terrestrial pause, or whether as past or still future, it is undeniable that if it prophesies a literal silence in heaven, it is spoken of as a most unusual event and of very short duration.

Revelation describes the communion of saints, there as here, to consist not merely of a vast congregation singing in perfect harmony the new song of Moses and the Lamb, nor of the multitude which no man can number bowing before the throne, offering each his individual worship, but also of souls calling one to another, imparting information and exciting others to new praise. They speak of personal perceptions, experiences and anticipations.

Recognition is an assumed necessity. It is a common observation of travellers that everywhere they find acquaintances. Strangers in conversation soon discover some connecting link—subjects of common interest, places which both have visited, experiences which have been similar, mutual friends, and often close blood relationships, if not former intimacies. This will be still more true in heaven. We shall not be distracted by the care of the body. We shall be relieved from the perplexities of business and the care of other things. Our communion will be uninterrupted and prolonged. We will delight in sympathy, and have no fear of being misunderstood or misrepresented. We will have the fullest confidence in each other and take special delight in each discovered tie which binds us closer to the members of the household of faith. The chief theme of heaven, in all our intercourse with God and each other, will be Redemption, not in the abstract nor in general, but in its personal application to us. We will praise Him " who was slain and has redeemed us to God by His own blood," " and has made us unto our God kings and priests."[1] As we render thanks before all, for Christian parents, for the seal of the covenant affixed in infancy, for those who taught us of Christ, led us to the cross, rejoiced at our conversion, helped us in duty, prayed for us in temptation, reclaimed us when wandering, were the means of our sanctification and efficiency, and stood by us when we were called into glory, there will gather round us those, for whom we give thanks, who will bless Christ that they had given, if "a cup of water only, in His name, to one of the least of His disciples."[2] While we recall our heart's desire and prayer to God that our kinsmen according to the flesh might be saved, and as we praise Christ for His love, which constrained us to declare His grace, the stars in the crown of our rejoicing and the seals of our ministry will

[1] Rev. v. 9, 10.   [2] Matt. x. 42; Mark ix. 41

gather, perhaps in unexpected numbers, to join in our thanksgiving and to recognize us as the means of their salvation. Forgotten faces, names, circumstances and conversations shall all be recalled. For memory is to be restored and made perfect. Our converse with these saints will be of past experiences in divine grace, present blessedness in Christ's presence and anticipated increase of knowledge of Him, of efficiency in His service and of delight in His worship. These are subjects which will be of mutual and absorbing interest, and will complete our recognition, render our friendships more intimate, and perfect our enjoyment of each other in the Lord.

If, then, speech, or communication in any form, be permitted between souls after death; if any reference to our earthly life be made in the hearing of others; if in our thanksgiving we speak of our spiritual experiences begun in the flesh, when we were helpers of each other's faith, causes of stumbling to some, deceived and being deceived, bearers of each other's burdens and co-laborers in the visible church, then recognition must be unavoidable. It is the natural and necessary result of speech, and will continually awaken new gratitude to Him who has wonderfully kept us unto salvation, and increased our love towards those who have helped us in the hour of temptation, or who have been saved through our instrumentality.

VII.

RECOGNITION BY SIGHT.

AT present, we depend upon the eye, more than any other bodily organ, for recognition. Yet the blind can develop the other senses to be almost as reliable. The footstep, voice, or the touch enable them to call each friend by name. In thinking of future meetings, we naturally expect to know each other by sight. But we are prompted at once to say, How can this be? All that we have seen of our friends is their bodily form, which will then be in the grave. Their souls we have never discerned, and, being spirits, they cannot be objects of sight.

This seems plausible. But the Scriptures speak of angels and other spirits, and of the souls under the altar as seen by each other, and even by men in the flesh. There can be therefore no impossibility nor improbability in the vision of spirits. They are immaterial, but it is a mistake to imagine that they are without forms. God is an infinite Spirit and fills immensity with His presence, and therefore can have no shape. We are forbidden to conceive of Him in a form, or to make any likeness or image of Him. To do so, is to deny His infinitude. But all angels and souls are finite. They are located, confined within certain limits, within which they are, and beyond which they are not. The most unsubstantial of earthly things have forms, definite each moment, however constantly changing— the cloud that presently vanishes away; the unseen vapor, whose deadly influence destroys the dog, but cannot affect the taller animal by its side. Spirits, being finite, must have forms. That these are definite and permanent, is everywhere assumed in Scripture, even in those passages which represent the spirit as taking for a time some shape that is not his own. The devil appears as an angel of light or as a serpent. Still he has his own proper form, which, indeed, may be very different from what in thought we usually ascribe to him. Angels have appeared as weary eastern travellers, clothed with human garments and with staves, and as young men in long white robes, and also, as we think, in their own form, with wings, with "countenance like lightning and raiment white as snow."[1]

This must also be true of the souls of men. That they have definite forms is the general

Matt. xxviii. 3

conviction of men in all ages and lands. They are called ghosts, shapes, shadows, etc., as indicating that they can be perceived by the senses. In all descriptions of their real or fancied appearances on earth, and of their condition in the spiritual world, there is, in this, a full agreement with the representations of the Word of God; that they are localized and have definite and permanent forms, by which they can be recognized and distinguished from others. Shakespeare describes Hamlet as seeing the distinct shape of his father's ghost, whose identity he could not question. To him and others it was "in the same figure like the king that's dead." Macbeth is so certain that Banquo's ghost was a reality, that he is made to say, "If I stand here, I saw him." "Saul discerned Samuel, either from personal observation, or from the witch's description: "an old man cometh up and he is covered with a mantle."[1] The saints, gathered in the house of Mary, the mother of John, praying, would not believe Rhoda, that Peter stood before the gate, but said, "It is his angel."[2] All these and like descriptions indicate that, according to popular opinion, the souls of the departed have definite forms, and, further, that these forms have a close resemblance to their physical frames. General convictions, not dependent upon education or local tradition, are seldom at fault. They have some common origin, as in an original communication from God or in the instincts of our nature. They are often confirmed by advancing science and by revelation. In this case the latest investigations of science seem to furnish an illustration of its truth.

In medical schools I have frequently seen

[1] I Sam. xxviii. 14.   [2] Acts xii. 15.

pictures of the same man, but variously presented. In one he appears in his natural condition, and in others the same outline is in turn filled with drawings of muscular tissues, of the ramifications of blood vessels, of the innumerable expansions of the nerve fibres, and of the lymphatic ducts. These pictures are, of course, very imperfect, yet they indicate that these various systems most minutely correspond to the same form. It is the skin only that we see, yet the slightest penetration of any part of it demonstrates, in the oozing blood, the shrinking from pain and the absorbing process instantly begun, that each of these other systems has been touched. Therefore, in our physical frames, we have many forms encased, all of which coincide to the same outward model. Indeed, as science advances, these are found to be still more numerous, and many of them are apparently approaching the immaterial or spiritual. There is the system of bioplasts, which change inorganic into living matter, and that influence which is unseen and cannot be analyzed, but which is transmitted to and fro by the nerves, and that mysterious life which pervades the whole body and extends to every part of its surface. Beside all this, there seems to be another and more spiritual form, that self-consciousness, or consciousness of self, which we all perceive. It is not confined to the brain—no one so imagines—much less to that point in it still undetermined, where mind and matter, soul and body, are said alone to touch. Conscious personality is not in a part, nor beyond the form of the body, but exactly conforms to it. This illustration is in part used by Rev. Archibald McCullagh, D. D., in his most admirable and comforting book, "Beyond the Stars," who in a measure quotes from Rev. Joseph Cook's work on biology.

All this illustrates, if it does not actually prove, that souls have the same forms, members, and features which distinguish their bodies, and therefore, when separated from the flesh, they can be recognized by all who have spiritual discernment. The Bible, as we have seen, in many places assumes this to be the fact. The Holy Ghost declares that "there are celestial bodies and bodies terrestrial, but the glory of the celestial is one, and the glory of the terrestrial is another."[1] This passage is of force, whether by celestial bodies is meant those of angels or of the souls of men. There are definite forms of celestial beings adapted to their heavenly existence, whose glory excels that of those who inhabit this earth. "There is a natural

[1] I Cor. xv. 40.

body, and there is a spiritual body."[1] There is a distinction between these, not as to form but as to nature. The one is material, adapted to our present life, and the other immaterial, fitted for a spiritual world. The revised version, in accord with the earliest manuscripts, reads, "if there is a natural body, there is also a spiritual body." The one is as certain as the other. There is a close connection between the two. In this, as in all other things, the seen is but the manifestation and expression of the unseen, the natural of the spiritual. It is admitted that Paul is speaking in this chapter of the resurrection body, its identity with that which is sown in corruption, and of its transformation like unto Christ's glorious body. But he is using illustrations showing that even now there are different kinds of bodies, as of

[1] I Cor. xv. 44.

sun, moon, and stars; of men, beasts, fishes and birds; of divers kinds of seed; and as a more close analogy he here refers to the natural and spiritual bodies which we now possess, the one seen and the other unseen. The laying aside of the outer form does not leave us destitute of figure, organs, and features.

We have spiritual bodies. " For which cause we faint not, but though our outward man perish, yet the inward man is renewed day by day.... For we know that if our earthly house of this tabernacle were dissolved, we have a building of God, an house not made with hands, eternal in the heavens. For in this we groan, earnestly desiring to be clothed upon with our house, which is from heaven. If so be that being clothed we shall not be found naked. For we which are in this tabernacle do groan, being burdened:

not for that we would be unclothed, but clothed upon, that mortality might be swallowed up of life."[1] Many suppose this passage refers to heaven and the mansions there prepared for us. But Paul is not speaking of locations or of our transportation from earth to heaven, but of a personal change, the dissolution of our fleshly tabernacles, the outward man, and of the continued possession of the building of God which is from heaven, the celestial body, the inward man. "If so be that being clothed we shall not be found naked."

As we shall see in the next chapter, there are causes which determine the personal peculiarities of our bodily forms. These causes are to be found in the immaterial part of our nature, which conforms the outward to the inward, the bodily to the spiritual. Our

[1] II Cor. iv. 16—v. 4.

present appearance is what it is because of our personal characteristics. If, therefore, our fleshly features express our inward nature, how much more are we to be spiritually modelled after the same image. The two forms expressing the same person and character, and determined by the same cause, must closely resemble each other. It is, therefore, reasonable that souls shall be visible, and can be easily recognized by those who have known them on earth. Changed they shall be, made more beautiful, and freed from all imperfections and defects, but they will be the same in all essential peculiarities. Moses' face, when he came down from the mount, shone with celestial glory, but his features were unaltered. We shall see and know the faces which have here gladdened our homes, and after which we have long yearned. There shall be on them no trace of sorrow or pain, no expression of worldliness or of conflict with sin. They will be radiant with joy, resplendent with holiness, reflecting the beauty of the Lord.

VIII.

RECOGNITION BY CHARACTER.

INTIMATELY connected with the subject of the last chapter is recognition by perception of character. If our spiritual forms shall resemble our corporeal, it is because there is some reason for our present peculiarities of shape and feature, which are essentially personal, and therefore permanent. A man's soul would be out of place in a woman's body, and we would feel exceedingly uncomfortable in any body but our own. This brings us to a fact which is becoming more clearly demonstrated. The physical is moulded by the spiritual. It has long been noticed that there is a close connection between the bodily appearance and the inward character. Even animals are attracted by some persons and terrified by others. An infant will study the face of a stranger, and quickly express confidence or firmly reject all possible overtures. Whatever may be our preconceived opinions of another's character, and however confirmed they may be by his reported conduct and speeches, they are verified or reversed when we look into his face. We are confident that a man with those features cannot be dishonest or cruel, and we as positively assert that another is capable of any crime and has revelled in wickedness.

It is not asserted that these judgments are always correct. Mistakes are often made, because hypocrites and dissemblers may assume appearances and expressions which are contrary to their real characters, and carefully refrain from manifesting emotions which strongly move them. We are finite, and liable to make mistakes. We are often careless in our inspection. The facts may be rightly discerned, but our conclusion may be false. The troubled brow may indicate perplexity how to do good as well as fear of being detected in evil. Indignation may be mistaken for anger, pity for a sneer, and self-respect for selfishness or pride. A passing feeling caused by sudden excitement may be regarded as a permanent trait of character. Sadness under a deep affliction may be judged to be habitual depression. Nevertheless these very mistakes verify the principle. It is because the face portrays character and reveals the inward purpose that hypocrites study to overcome the natural impulse to manifest in lip and eye their nature and designs, and to assume expressions which are entirely foreign to them, or to their moods. And it is because we know that the outward manner is by a constant law of nature determined by the inward emotion, that even our mistaken conclusions have an influence over us which we can hardly resist. We feel justified in believing that there is a heavy heart behind the overshadowed face, even when we misjudge the cause of sorrow. A smile may deceive, but we are certain that it ought to indicate a passing pleasure or a kindly disposition.

It may be said that the outward manner, after all, only reveals the present thoughts and feelings. But thoughts and emotions, however fleeting, are determined by permanent traits of character. The snap of a dog shows his disposition and we know he should never be trusted. The glance of an eye demonstrates that love or hatred dwells in the heart, and may be at any moment evoked. And these passing expressions of permanent characteristics necessarily become habits. Frequent smiles make a cheerful countenance. Indulged suspicions surround the person with an air of distrust. And these have a reflexed action, developing those traits which are often expressed. The face photographs that which passes within, and these views become fixed, leaving a permanent record on the features. Many a son has read the whole story of his mother's broken heart in the deep lines which disappointment, anxiety and grief have traced on her countenance. Every man's inner history is thus recorded, as a warrior's conflicts are written in his many scars. A dude cannot look like a man of business. A student differs in appearance from a day laborer. An upright man cannot be mistaken for a drunken debauchee. The very forms of features indicate traits of character. The chin of a certain formation reveals firmness and persistency of purpose. A high forehead shows intellectual ability. The shape of the head manifests mental and even moral traits. There is a real foundation for phrenology. Wrong conclusions are often drawn from observed facts—that the physical peculiarities determine the intellectual and that a man's future may be thus forecast. Whereas the reverse is true, the mental traits, both hereditary and acquired, are the causes of the conformation of the brain and skull, and show what the man has been and is. Even moral changes, produced by the inward work of the Holy Ghost, are discerned in the outward man. These are so clearly marked that frequently they cannot be mistaken. Peace with God, joy in His fellowship, and holy interest in man, are manifested, to the surprise of former companions. The disfigurements of past years of sin are not immediately, perhaps never, wholly eradicated, but a decided change has evidently taken place, and a new attractiveness or charm has been imparted. The golden bowl has been burnished, although marks of past abuse are still apparent.

In proportion, therefore, as we know the real character of a friend, we perceive the reason for his bodily appearance. We closely connect the two in thought. We are troubled, if we find any dissimilarity; and are confirmed in our opinion when we perceive the harmony. As we read of historical persons we form distinct conceptions of their appearance, not merely as possible but as necessary. If these conceptions differ from those formed by others, it is only because our idea of the characters is not what others have apprehended.

Each has obtained a partial view, and therefore there is a variety in our ideas of their personal appearances, but the variety is chiefly in details. There is a general agreement. In the several groups of historical personages who are engaged in the same work and animated by a like spirit, we individualize each. Luther, Calvin and Knox had much in com mon, lived in the same age, were bold in the defence of the same truth, employed similar means, and manifested a determined opposition to Rome, a love for the Church of Christ and a desire for salvation of men, yet their peculiarities were so marked that no one imagines that they resembled each other. Moses and Elias were both miracle workers, leaders of the people, teachers of duty enforced by terrible threatenings, and prophets and types of Christ, yet the disciples on the Mount of Transfiguration had no difficulty in identifying the law-giver, or in recognizing the fearless reformer. Peter, James and John were apostles, and stood together, as the chosen three, always near their Master. Yet no one would mistake Peter for one of the sons of thunder, nor take James for the beloved disciple, the seer of the Revelation. When we shall see " Abraham and Isaac and Jacob and all the prophets in the kingdom of God," as we apprehend their several characters we shall have no difficulty in distinguishing them. When our loved ones receive us into everlasting habitations, we shall be surprised at their freedom from sin and defects, and at their wonderful development in grace, but the well remembered characteristics—of tastes, talents, activities and aspirations, must reveal each one's personality. When we behold Christ we shall know Him—not so much because of His session on the throne, the homage rendered to Him or the exceeding brightness of His countenance, but because in His features we shall behold what no painting has ever represented—the fulness of the Godhead bodily, the inherent perfection of divine attributes in human form, in His glory "the chiefest among ten thousand," and, to each redeemed soul, "the one altogether lovely."[1]

Not unfrequently we recognize others without personal contact, merely by some known peculiarity. In a picture gallery we not only judge of the character of each artist by his choice of subjects and manner of treating them, but we perceive that there are characteristics which run through his works, by which all his paintings can be identified. These peculiarities manifest traits of character, tastes and skill. As we study the various productions of each, we can also

[1] Song of Solomon, v. 10-16.

often determine the succession in which they were painted, and mark his improvement, and the formation and development of his style. They record the full history of his artistic life. A lover of music can recognize the composer of the harmony which thrills him if he has carefully studied any of his pieces. Authors are known by their style of composition, and their grasp and expression of thought. Isaiah, Jeremiah, and Daniel, in revealing the future of the Church, have left their own characteristics in their writings, in which, also, are evidences that they were moved by the Holy Ghost. Matthew, Mark, Luke, and John have presented their personal conceptions of the gospel of the Son of God, and their peculiar relations to Christ. We can even perceive the presence and influence of Peter in what Mark has written, and of Paul as Luke " set forth in order a declaration of those things which are most surely believed."[1] We recognize most of our correspondents without glancing at the signatures affixed to their letters. Trains of thought we know can come only from one gifted mind. The manner of showing emotions often reveals the personality. A mother knows at once which child has placed a rose on her table, or labored in some house task, or anticipated an unexpressed desire. These acts of love have been done according to the peculiar disposition of each child, and she makes no mistake. All these special talents, tastes, and emotions are personal, belonging to the inner man, and are independent of outward circumstances; they are, therefore, permanent and shall be unaffected by death. We shall be greeted in heaven by parents as by none other. The welcome of father will differ from that of mother, as these

[1] Luke i.

differed on earth. Children and friends will all, there as here, express their characters, tastes and powers in their own ways, and be recognized thereby. This, indeed, is the highest and most satisfactory method of recognition.

It may, however, be said that marvellous changes shall take place in character after death, and that the changes will probably advance with wonderful rapidity. So that while we have been finishing our course on earth, our loved ones have been entirely transformed. This is true, yet it is to be noticed that the change is twofold. (1.) An entire freedom from sin. But very much of the sin whereby our loved ones are defiled is unknown to us. It is perceived fully only by the Searcher of hearts. Much has not been reported to us, much has never been confessed, and we have failed to suspect the evil which has been apparent to others. What we have perceived we have excused, labored to counteract, and watched as it was being supplanted by growing virtues. We have in love, and in faith in God's covenant, cherished ideal conceptions of our children and friends—what they would be, and certainly shall be, without these defects and sins. It will not be so much a surprise when we behold them perfected by grace. Every line in a child's first sketch may be wrong, but it is still the same drawing after it has been corrected under the direction of the master. We, who now behold our children with faith and love, and all others with Christian charity, will not be so much surprised to find them without the faults which now we ignore. We are accustomed to regard sin as the result of temptations from the world, flesh, and devil, and often imagine what others would be with a holy environment and where no temptation assails, but where God's love is the all controlling motive, and where saints and angels exercise their holy influence. Throughout our whole Christian experience we have been depending upon the Spirit's wonderful power to subdue sin and perfect sanctification in us and others. We rest upon Christ's promise that we shall all be without spot or blemish. We long with confidence for the fulfilment in ourselves, and expect its realization in others.

(2.) There will be also a perfecting in holiness. Here faults often conceal virtues, and graces, even the most essential, scarcely appear, or are dwarfed and marred in their growth. The change will be wonderful when there shall be no concealment, when each grace shall be present and in full development. Yet it is a development, not a transformation. Holiness is not to us an unknown attribute. The Christian graces, which will constitute the glory of the saints, are, indeed, divine, but they have been planted in an earthly garden, and we have seen each grow in human hearts. New seeds from distant climes may astonish us at every stage of their strange development. But we have been long familiar with the word which has been planted in our hearts, and we have watched "first the blade, then the ear, and after that the full corn in the ear."[1] We have often seen the whole process until the fruits of the Spirit are brought forth: "love, joy, peace, long-suffering, gentleness, goodness, faith, meekness, temperance."[2] We have seen great variety of developments, but of the same graces. In some we have beheld one or more of these brought almost to perfection.

[1] Mark iv. 28. [2] Gal. v. 22, 23.

And there is not one divine grace which is not to be found fully manifested in Jesus Christ, "for in Him dwelleth the fulness of the Godhead bodily."[1] We know Him and "are to be changed into His image."[2] We have, therefore, some conception of the perfect sanctification carried on in heaven. Nor will this perfecting of the saints obliterate all distinction. "One star differeth from another star in glory."[3] Peter and John were very different as fishermen, as disciples the contrast was as strong, as apostles and aged saints they retained their striking individualities, and in glory they must reflect each in his own manner the beauty of the Lord, and glorify Him in different stations and services. And the peculiarities of Christian talents and characters which distinguish our friends here, will be noticeable there. Their special

[1] Col. ii. 9. [2] II Cor. iii. 18. [3] I Cor. xv. 41.

adaptation for their present work will be more apparent when engaged in that for which they are now preparing. The skill and delicacy in handling of tools by an apprentice causes his master to look for him in after life among those whose nice carving creates admiration, but his companion, as good a workman, will be sought among those whose frames for buildings and bridges may be depended upon. The Captain of our salvation is now preparing each Christian for his office and service in the ranks of his hosts above. As we know them while in training, we shall recognize them in that unnumbered multitude by their developed powers and peculiarities. Mary will find undisturbed delight at Christ's feet, hearing His words, and Martha will serve Him with unwearied activity. They will be recognized by these traits, yet Mary will be more communicative and Martha more receptive. Dr. A. A. Hodge, in his "popular lectures," says, "The recognition of friends then will not be the recognition of souls through the remembered features of the body, but rather the recognition of persons through irradiating characteristics of their souls. When we rise on that great Easter morning, and our new senses sweep the historic generations of the redeemed, we will know the great masters of thought and song, and the great leaders of the sacramental hosts in instant glance, from our long knowledge of their thoughts and deeds. And when in the centre of the hosts we meet the Object to which all thoughts and hearts converge, there will be no need of introduction between the glorified Lord and his glorified servant, however humble he may be. The instant, rapturous recognition will be mutual and spontaneous: Rabboni! Mary!"

IX.

RECOGNITION THROUGH OTHERS

THERE have been cases of long absences —as of children stolen from their parents, brought up under strange circumstances, and developed under influences foreign to their birth—in which recognition would seem almost impossible. A child of refined parents has lived until manhood among savages, or a peasant's babe has been reared as the prince for whom he had been substituted. In such cases the ordinary methods of identification and recognition, which we have considered, are of no avail. Sight can discern nothing in "the Ruler of all Egypt" that bears the slightest resemblance to the lad sold to the Ishmaelites. The conversation which took place between Joseph and his brethren on business, or at the feast in his house, gave no suspicion of his identity. The character manifested by him was so unlike the " dreamer of dreams " and the favorite of his father, that they could not believe his most positive assurance. When, after forty years, Moses returned to Egypt, he was unrecognized. The long period had produced great changes in his appearance, and the protracted discipline had transformed the violent revenger into the meekest of men. His work of deliverance was thereafter effected, not by his violence or political influence, but as the mouthpiece of Jehovah and by the miraculous power of God. In the case of Joseph, he was gradually made known to his brethren by his speech in their tongue, and by his knowledge of their names and of the details of their early life. The Israelites recognized their deliverer through God's testimony by miracles. But more frequently some mutual friend, like Barnabas, must testify of the experiences of a Saul, his wonderful transformation of character, and his zeal and activity in the common cause. This is especially necessary when the separation has been long, when it began from early childhood and when the change in character is very decided. Shakspeare has rightly described the testimony of the old shepherd as essential that Perdita had been constantly under his care, since he found her a babe on the shore with the evidences of her birth.

The changes wrought in eternity are marvellous and advance with strange rapidity. The infant of a few days develops more perfectly under Christ's nurture than those who have grown up under our guidance. We think of our child as a babe, because taken from our arms almost as soon as we had embraced him, but he has matured more rapidly than his brothers, and beyond our own possible development on earth. We received the child from the Lord. We consecrated him to God. We claimed His promise to us and to our seed. When He called the little one to Himself, we said, "It is the Lord, let him do as seemeth Him good."[1] He encouraged us to say, "I shall go to him, but he shall not return to me."[2] When therefore the Lord "shall come to receive us also to Himself,"[3] it is according to Scripture to believe that He will present to us the child whom He has enriched with all His covenanted glory. When "the angels shall carry us into Abraham's bosom,"[4] they

[1] I Sam. iii. 18.   [2] II Sam. xii. 23.
[3] John xiv. 3.   [4] Luke xvi. 22.

will bring us to those of the household of faith who by providence and grace have been most intimately identified with us. When "we shall see Abraham, Isaac and Jacob, and all the prophets in the Kingdom of God,"[1] each one will be made known unto us. Our natures remaining essentially the same, we will, in our communion with saints, long after those who have preceded us into glory. If neither eye, nor ear, nor perception of character will enable us to discern them in the happy throng, ministering angels and saints will bring the loved ones and tell us of the experiences and methods by which they have attained their perfection.

All this would naturally be expected, were it God's will that our present human relationships be continued hereafter. It may be said, however, that Christ has intimated that such

[1] Luke xiii. 28.

is not His will. " The children of this world marry and are given in marriage, but they which shall be accounted worthy to obtain that world, and the resurrection from the dead, neither marry nor are given in marriage; neither can they die any more, for they shall be equal unto the angels, and are the children of God, being the children of the resurrection."[1] We should notice, however, that Christ is here speaking of marriage as a divine ordinance for the raising up of seed. In that world there is to be no increase by births nor decrease by death. In this respect the saints shall be equal to angels. He does not deny that present intimacies are to be continued. Relationships exist among the angels. They are not indeed like men set in families. They are placed in ranks, associated in similar service, and co-

[1] Luke xx. 34-36.

operate in long-continued joint work. They are brought in peculiar relations to the elect as ministering spirits; to infants—"in heaven their angels do always behold the face of My Father which is in heaven;" and to nations, as revealed in the prophecy of Daniel. In the book of Revelation they are described as holding peculiar relations to the Elders, to the souls under the altar, to each other, and in reference to the last plagues, anti-Christ, Babylon, lost men and wicked spirits.

The relationships among men are very multiform. The text does not deny this. It refers only to one—that of marriage, and this only as designed for the procreation of children, which it says in that respect shall not be continued. Elsewhere it is asserted that all human relations were ordained to reveal those spiritual and permanent ones which we maintain toward God and toward each other.

Almost all we know, of our standing with God, our union with Christ, our connection with the Holy Ghost, our association with each other and all saints, and of the plan of salvation and the methods of its application, has been illustrated and typified by our present relations with each other.

And the intimacies of heaven are symbolized in the same manner. The covenant founded on the connection between parents and their children is God's favorite method of declaring and transmitting His grace. By cherishing in us a special interest toward our children according to the flesh, He secures continuous and self-denying efforts to bring them to faith and godliness. To faithful parents He has made promises, spiritual and eternal. To obedient children, He has pledged long life in the land, only as the evidence of an unending inheritance in the real Canaan. The spiritual are the true seed of Abraham, but there is an emphasis laid also upon the seed according to the flesh, who, when also spiritual, shall be more glorious and beloved than those who are begotten only by faith. We are so taught in Romans xi. 12–24 : "If the fall of them be the riches of the world, and the diminishing of them the riches of the Gentiles, how much more their fulness?" "If the casting away of them be the reconciling of the world, what shall the receiving of them be but life from the dead?" "God is able to graft them in again." "How much more shall these which be the natural branches, be grafted into their own olive tree?" These human relationships were designed as types. If they represent a permanent union with Christ, they must also be permanent. If they exhibit temporary affinities, they will remain as long as Christ continues in those attitudes. Such is the conclusion taught by reason and the plan of God. Throughout the Old Testament men were set apart as sacrificers, to present bloody offerings in behalf of the people unto the Lord, because through all those ages Christ was preparing Himself and His people for " offering of the body of Jesus Christ once for all." [1] But this being accomplished, He ceased to be a sacrificer. " After He had offered one sacrifice for sin, forever, He sat down on the right hand of God." [2] There can therefore be no more priests among men. He continues " to reconcile us to God," [3] and there are ambassadors who pray you in Christ's stead, " be ye reconciled to God." [4] He makes " continual inter cession for us " [5]—and we are exhorted " that first of all, supplications, intercessions and

[1] Heb. x. 10.   [2] Heb. x. 12.   [3] Eph. 11. 16.
[4] II Cor. v. 20.   [5] Heb. vii. 25.

giving of thanks be made for all men."[1] The relationships which are expressed by the Fatherhood of God, the brotherhood of Christ, and the fellowship of the Holy Ghost are permanent. They are described as not in any way identified with our stay on earth. They are not fully realized here. Our Father is in heaven. We are co-heirs of an inheritance yet to be revealed. And the Spirit does not now testify of Himself. We have only a foretaste, a dim conception, of our union with the triune God. Until all this be fully realized throughout eternity, the types, our human relationships, must continue. There shall be the true "seed of Abraham," "the twelve tribes of Israel," fathers and their children to many generations, brothers and fellow laborers. And these will forever reveal to us the intimacy of our union with God.

[1] I Tim. ii. 1.

Indeed some of these types have no real fulfilment in this life. The marriage of the Lamb shall not take place until, "the first heaven and the first earth have passed away," until all the elect have been gathered, and "the new Jerusalem, coming down from God out of heaven, has been prepared as a bride adorned for her husband."[1] It would seem therefore that the marriage relationship, in its highest conception of perfect love, confidence, sympathy and helpfulness, shall continue and forever reveal the fulness of our union with Christ.

It is then the will of God that these relationships shall be perpetual. It is not merely fleshly instinct, but a divinely implanted principle, which leads us to long after our loved ones, to be gathered to our fathers, and to see again the children which God has

[1] Rev. xxi. 1, 2.

graciously given us and who shall forever rise up and call us blessed. And it is to be expected that God, the angels and the saints will renew our relationships to those from whom we are now separated, and bring us to those whom we would not otherwise have readily recognized. Rev. Archibald Alexander, D. D., in his "Religious Experience," Chapter XXII, says, "As here knowledge is acquired by the aid of instructors, why may not the same be the fact in heaven? What a delightful employment to the saints who have been drinking in the knowledge of God and His works for thousands of years to communicate instruction to the saints just arrived! How delightful to conduct the pilgrim, who has just finished his race, through the ever blooming bowers of paradise, and to introduce him to this and the other ancient believer, and to assist him to find out and recognize, among so great a multitude, old friends and earthly relatives. There need be no dispute about our knowing, in heaven, those whom we knew and loved here; for if there should be no faculty by which they could at once be recognized, yet by extended and familiar intercouse with the celestial inhabitants, it cannot be otherwise but that interesting discoveries will be made continually; and the unexpected recognition of old friends may be one of the sources of pleasure which will render heaven so pleasant."

X.

RECOGNITION BY OTHER MEANS.

WE have now considered four methods by which souls after death may be recognized. Any one of these may be employed and would render us certain as to the identity of our friends. Often two or more means will be used, and thus increase the certainty. We may be introduced by angels or saints; and at first accept without hesitation the delightful assurance. But soon, as here on earth, the features, however changed, will reveal traces of the face we have long cherished, and we will more and more perceive that it is the very same, developed and sanctified. As we converse, familiar peculiarities of thought and expression will be recognized, and joint experiences will be recalled, until the long separation seems insignificant. As we draw nearer to each other our inward characteristics will reveal themselves, former misunderstandings will be removed, and the real personality of each will be more apparent in our renewed intimacy. Much of our ever-increasing joy in the communion of saints and of our loved ones, will consist in this increasing recognition and ever clearer appreciation of each other's characters, as beautified and perfected by divine grace.

All this would be true, were we to possess only present known faculties, developed and made unerring. We have reason, however, to believe that new powers will be granted to us, of which we now, of course, can form no conception. A blind man may hear labored descriptions of sight and of the beauties by which he is unconsciously surrounded. No illustrations can enable him to form any conception of the closed avenue of sense nor of the vast fields of beauty to which it leads. The servant of the prophet had no idea of the spiritual forces by which they were protected. He saw only the mighty hosts of the Syrians which compassed the city. But when Elisha prayed and spiritual perception was given, "He beheld the mountains full of horses and chariots of fire round about Elisha."[1] The caterpillar knows not what organs he will have when as a butterfly he comes from the cocoon. When we lay aside the earthly and enter upon our heavenly state, new faculties will doubtless be added to our present senses, by which other means of acquiring knowledge, and new wonders shall

[1] II Kings vi. 17.

be opened to us. By these new faculties and powers we will also perceive and recognize our friends. Perhaps even here at times we receive impressions through organs not yet developed. Sometimes we become conscious of the presence of a friend, when none of our five senses has been or could be exercised. He has entered a crowded room, silent and out of sight, but we perceive his entrance and approach. In a large assembly we discern one with whom we desire to speak. As we earnestly look at him, and are eager for his attention, he knows not why he is uncomfortable, irritable, and nervously conscious that he is wanted, until he raises his eyes and meets our gaze. We can not explain this, nor many other methods by which some persons obtain and receive information, yet we can not deny the fact. They seem to be intimations of means of recognition and communication, which shall be more direct and reliable than our bodily senses and the powers now exercised through them. And of this we may be sure, each new faculty for obtaining information will increase our knowledge of each other's persons, characters, and histories, and thus aid our mutual recognition.

XI.

RESURRECTION.

THE resurrection of the body will greatly change our condition. Those who shall at the time be on earth, shall also pass at once into the resurrection state. "We which are alive and remain unto the coming of the Lord shall not prevent them which are asleep. For the Lord Himself shall descend from heaven with a shout, with the voice of the archangel and with the trump of God: and the dead in Christ shall rise first; then we which are alive and remain shall be caught up together with them in the clouds to meet the Lord in the air, and so shall we ever be with the Lord."[1] "We shall all be changed, in a moment, in the twinkling of an eye, at the last trump; for the trumpet shall sound, and the dead shall be raised, and we shall be changed."[2] We must therefore consider what effect will the resurrection have upon recognition.

That there will be a resurrection there can be no doubt. Christ tells us that it was revealed in the first books of the Bible. The plainest declaration in the Old Testament is in Daniel: "Many of them that sleep in the dust of the earth shall awake, some to everlasting life and some to shame and everlasting contempt."[3] But Isaiah, Hosea and Ezekiel speak almost as clearly: "Thy dead men shall live, together with my dead body shall they arise."[4] "I will ransom them from the

[1] I Thess. iv. 15-17.   [2] I Cor. xv. 51, 52.
[3] Dan. xii. 2.   [4] Is. xxvi. 19.

power of the grave, I will redeem them from death: O death, I will be thy plague. O grave, I will be thy destruction." [1]

At the time of Christ the two great parties among the Jews were the Pharisees and the Sadducees. The former held the doctrine of the resurrection, and the latter denied and ridiculed it. Christ in His disputations with them said to the Sadducees, " Ye therefore do greatly err,"[2] while He confirmed the teaching of the Pharisees. The apostles from the first laid special stress upon the resurrection of the body. Paul tells us that everything depends upon this. " If there be no resurrection of the dead, then is Christ not risen. And if Christ be not risen, then is our preaching vain, and your faith is also vain." " For if the dead rise not, then is not Christ raised, and if Christ be not raised, your faith is vain; ye are

[1] Hos. xiii. 14.   [2] Mark xii. 24-27.

yet in your sins; then they also which are fallen asleep in Christ are perished."[1] The object of the resurrection of Christ, its connection with redemption, its relation to our faith, and its effect upon our bodies, are matters of great moment and interest. But we are concerned at present only with the facts. Christ did rise from the dead, and there is to be a general resurrection at the last day. These two facts are here declared to be beyond doubt, and indisputable. They involve each other. If there be no resurrection, Christ has not risen. If he has, then we also shall rise. If He rose literally, so shall we. In the previous verses, some of the many infallible proofs are presented, that "He rose the third day, according to the Scriptures," and was seen and recognized by the apostles, singly and in companies, and "after that by

[1] I Cor. xv. 13-18.

above five hundred brethren at once." [1] The resurrection of Christ being thus established, there can be no question nor doubt that there will be a general resurrection at the last day.

The resurrection is sometimes used to denote that marvellous transformation effected in the soul by the application of redemption by the quickening Spirit, and also to describe the consummation of the spiritual kingdom of Christ. It is however true, that a literal resurrection of these bodies has been promised and will be effected. Redemption is not partial, but complete. Man is composed of soul and body. As such he sinned and came under the curse which affected both parts of his nature. As such also he is saved, and must be acquitted at the last day and received into the glory purchased by the blood of Christ. His soul pardoned, cleansed, and

[1] I Cor. xv. 3–8.

delivered, would be only a half triumph of Christ, and a partial salvation to man, if the other part of his nature were left under the destroying power of sin, death, and the devil. In this life we experience much of spiritual regeneration and sanctification, but "we which have the first fruits of the Spirit, even we ourselves groan within ourselves, waiting for the adoption, to wit, the redemption, of our body." "Because the creature itself also shall be delivered from the bondage of corruption into the glorious liberty of the children of God."[1]

The terms used indicate that a bodily as well as a spiritual resurrection is promised. Indeed that which is taught by the type must be true of the type as well as of the antitype. If water means spiritual purification, it must be physically cleansing. If leaven indicates the progress of the kingdom of heaven in the

[1] Rom. viii. 21-23.

soul, it must have the power to leaven the whole lump. And if resurrection represents the awaking of the soul from the death of sin to eternal life, there must be a rising of the body from the grave and corruption to new life and activity. The terms used in Scripture necessarily predict a literal resurrection of the body, whatever may be their spiritual signification. Care is taken to specify those things which are connected with the body. Thus, "Thy dead men shall live, together with my dead body shall they arise. Awake and sing ye that dwell in the dust, for thy dew is as the dew of herbs, and the earth shall cast out the dead."[1] "And many of them that sleep in the dust of the earth shall awake, some to everlasting life, and some to shame and everlasting contempt."[2] "Marvel not at this, for the hour is coming in the which all

[1] Is. xxvi. 19.   [2] Dan. xii. 2.

that are in the graves shall hear His voice and shall come forth."¹ "Now is Christ risen from the dead and become the first fruits of them that slept."² "So also is the resurrection of the dead. It is sown in corruption, it is raised in glory. It is sown in weakness, it is raised in power. It is sown a natural body, it is raised a spiritual body. There is a natural body, and there is a spiritual body."³ That which is sown, is raised. This is true of almost every text which speaks of the resurrection.

The objections answered by Christ and by Paul were concerning the literal raising of these bodies. The difficulties are not ignored nor explained away. What is impossible with men, is possible with God. The infinite God can accomplish that which He has promised. " God giveth it a body as it hath

---

[1] John v. 29. [2] I Cor. xv. 20. [3] 1 Cor. xv. 42-44.

pleased Him, and to every seed his own body."[1] The illustration which the Holy Ghost uses is very apt. The seed is imperfect, its real character undeveloped, and its beauty and use unknown, until it passes through decomposition. "It is not quickened except it die." If sown, "it bears grain, it may chance of wheat or of some other grain." This last state is far more important and beautiful than the former. There are great changes, but it is a continuation of the same seed, a literal resurrection of the same, a development of that which was contained in the seed. "So also is the resurrection of the dead."[2]

All scientific and other objections received the same solution. "Is the Lord's hand waxed short? Thou shalt see now whether my word shall come to pass unto thee or not."[3] "Is my hand shortened at all, that it cannot

[1] Cor. xv. 38.   [2] I Cor. xv. 36–42.   [3] Num. xi. 23

redeem? or have I no power to deliver? Behold, at my rebuke I dry up the sea, I make the rivers a wilderness: .... I clothe the heavens with blackness, and I make sackcloth their covering."[1] Can He redeem the soul, but be unable to restore the body? We are fools. The utmost of our knowledge is folly, compared with God's wisdom, and even with what we shall ourselves attain unto. We are very feeble. What is to us an absolute impossibility is accomplished as He speaks, at His touch. Shall we then judge that to be untrue which He has declared, or shall we set bounds to His ability to accomplish what He has promised? "Heaven and earth shall pass away, but My words shall not pass away."[2] "And I saw the dead, small and great, stand before God, and the books were opened, and another book was opened, which is the book

[1] Is. l. 2, 3. [2] Matt. xxiv. 35.

of life, and the dead were judged out of those things which were written in the books, according to their works. And the sea gave up the dead which were in it, and death and hell delivered up the dead which were in them, and they were judged every man according to their works."[1]

Some Christians do not want to believe in the doctrine of the resurrection. The body is the cause of much discomfort. It is a weight and drag upon the soul, the channel through which temptations come, the means by which sins have been committed, and the irresistible hindrance in every effort to do good. It is full of ailments, weakness, diseases, pain, and sometimes of long continued agony. From its torture, death is a relief. Many become impatient to be delivered from it, and when delivered, they want no more of it.

[1] Rev. xx. 12, 13.

They anticipate with pleasure the rapidity of motion of the disembodied soul, the freedom from sickness and suffering, and the liberty from the limitations of the few and feeble senses. The spirit life of angels is attractive, and after the enjoyment of spiritual liberty and activity for ages, the idea of a return to these miserable bodies is not a pleasant thought.

This is not the true doctrine of the resurrection. The Scriptures, while declaring that these same bodies shall be raised, as plainly describe the marvellous changes which shall take place in them, as they come from the graves, and as the living shall in a moment, in the twinkling of an eye, be changed. They will be beautified and adapted to the new environment, mode of existence, services and joy of the glorified souls. So far from being hindrances, they will greatly increase the means of activity and happiness of the redeemed. The body of Elijah is no clog to him in heaven. He and Enoch are represented as far more highly favored and as holding a more enviable position than the disembodied souls. Even the body of our Lord is described as "glorious." Its possession is part of His exaltation.

After the resurrection "God shall wipe all tears from their eyes; and there shall be no more death, neither sorrow, nor crying, neither shall there be any more pain, for the former things are passed away."[1] The description of the New Jerusalem, the bride, the Lamb's wife, is indeed that of the dwelling place of the saints, but it is more especially of the perfection of the redeemed who enter there. "He who hath builded the house hath more honor than the house."[2] The city

[1] Rev. xxi. 4.   [2] Heb. iii. 3.

which is so resplendent can be inhabited only by those who are far more beautiful. The changes to be wrought in these bodies are described as very great. Like the seed which becomes a plant bearing grain. They are to be raised " in incorruption," " in glory," " in power," " spiritual bodies," " bearing the image of the heavenly." Of this then we may be assured. Our resurrection bodies will be perfectly adapted to our condition and service in heaven, that their possession will advance us in our spiritual development and glory, and render us more capable of enjoyment and service.

XII.

THE RESURRECTION BODY.

AT first it may seem that we can form no adequate idea of the resurrection body. Nothing is said of that of Enoch. The record is short. All others died, "And Enoch walked with God, and he was not, for God took him."[1] Elijah went up by a whirlwind into heaven in a chariot of fire and horses of fire.[2] And he was seen with Moses on the Mount of Transfiguration. We learn only that his body was adapted to his glorified condition. At the crucifixion "The graves were opened and many bodies of the saints

[1] Gen. v. 24.   [2] II Kings ii. 11.

which slept arose, and came out of their graves, after His resurrection, and went into the holy city, and appeared unto many." [1] These were evidently actual bodies, belonging to individual saints. They came from their graves, could walk on the earth, and enter Jerusalem, yet like spirits "appear" unto many. From the descriptions of the last day we gather no further information than that in the body every man shall stand before Christ and be judged concerning the deeds done in the flesh, and that such will be the nature of the bodies of the saints and of the wicked, that they shall meet the Lord in the air.

Most of the terms used to describe the resurrection body are either indefinite or negative. "It is raised in glory" and "in power." "The dead shall be raised incorruptible, and we shall be changed. For this

[1] Matt. xxvii. 52. 53.

corruptible must put on incorruption, and this mortal must put on immortality," [1] not subject to decay and death. Yet these terms indicate a marvellous superiority of the resurrection body, although we may not be able to define the expressions "glory," "power." We notice that they are often used to describe the perfections of angels and even of God Himself. And they must therefore indicate high exaltation and beauty. The negative terms deny to our future body every thing that now mars them, renders them unattractive, or interferes with their activity. They shall not be subject to corruption or to death. Yet they are the same. " This corruptible must put on incorruption, and this mortal must put on immortality."

Other terms seem at first contradictory, and irreconcilably so. " A spiritual body."

[1] I Cor. xv. 43, 52, 53.

"There is a natural body and there is a spiritual body." "That was not first which is spiritual, but that which is natural, and afterward that which is spiritual."[1] These expressions, however, deserve and will repay careful study. They will also confirm much that we have already ascertained. "A natural body" of course means the body which we have now on earth. And a "spiritual body" describes that which we shall have after the resurrection. This is evident from the whole chapter. It is one and the same body. At first it is natural, and then, at the resurrection, it shall be spiritual. Nothing, perhaps, can be conceived as more opposite and irreconcilable in their properties than spirit and body. If these are by the Holy Ghost combined to give us a conception of the resurrection bodies, it is evident that

[1] I Cor. xv. 44-46.

they must possess qualities very diverse. They must have those which belong to the body and those which characterize the spirit. As bodies they are material, composed of parts, subject to the laws of nature, can be seen and handled, have organs of perception, can walk, eat and drink, and come into contact with other material objects. As spirits they appear and disappear, vanish out of sight, move with incredible velocity, are not dependent upon the laws of nature, do not need earthly food, cannot be confined nor excluded by walls, can assemble in the air and ascend to the highest heavens with all the freedom of angels and other pure spirits; they experience no fatigue, and therefore need not sleep; they are not liable to disease or injury, neither are they enfeebled by age. They are not hampered nor limited in their development, but are perfect manifestations of character, feeling and state.

It may be difficult for us to conceive of these opposite characteristics as belonging to the same object, the resurrection body. Yet, practically there is very little trouble when this description is applied to special cases. Those whom Christ raised from the dead— the ruler's daughter, the widow's son, and Lazarus at Bethany—were not awakened to resurrection but restoration to life, and so was Dorcas. They were brought back to continue their probation, to grow in stature, be a comfort to parents and sisters, to finish their appointed work on earth and to die once more. But in the cases before mentioned the bodies were spiritualized, and ascended to heaven to die no more. The body of Enoch "was not, for God took him."[1]

[1] Gen. v. 24.

He vanished, as did the angels when they ceased speaking to the patriarchs. Elijah went up into heaven, he "appeared" with the soul of Moses, and disappeared in the cloud which overshadowed them. The saints which came out of their graves could walk as men in the flesh, enter by the gates into Jerusalem, and as spirits "appear" unto many, and be no more seen on earth.

Of course the most perfect exhibition of the resurrection body is that of our Lord. It must not be supposed that His was an exceptional case. Before death His body was like ours in every respect. It was born, increased in stature, was weary, hungered and thirsted, was liable to pain and to death. When He bowed His head and gave up the ghost, the physical symptoms were the very same as in other men. He was laid in the tomb with spices, "as the manner of the

Jews is to bury,"[1] and His body was subject to the universal laws of the dead. And He rose in the same manner as we shall rise at the last day. Such is the argument in I Corinthians xv. The only distinction that can be made is concerning the power by which He rose. "I lay down my life, that I might take it again. No man taketh it from Me, but I lay it down of Myself. I have power to lay it down and I have power to take it again."[2] We are to be raised by Him. "For the hour is coming in the which all that are in the graves shall hear His voice, and shall come forth; they that have done good unto the resurrection of life, and they that have done evil unto the resurrection of damnation."[3] His body was in all respects like ours. He was born, lived, died, was buried, and rose, as all other men must. If there be no resur-

[1] John xix. 40. [2] John x. 17, 18. [3] John v. 28, 29

rection for men, there could be none for Him.

He is called, also, "the first fruits of them that slept." The first fruits were offered not only in a thanksgiving for the expected harvest, but also as an evidence and sample of that which was ready to be reaped. Christ's resurrection body assures us that we shall not be left in the grave, and reveals to us the kind of body "with which we shall come." This seems to be an unavoidable conclusion. We are not therefore surprised to read that "as we have borne the image of the earthy, we shall also bear the image of the heavenly."[1] "We look for the Saviour, the Lord Jesus Christ, who shall change our vile body that it may be fashioned like unto His glorious body, according to the working whereby He is able even to subdue all things unto

[1] I Cor. xv. 49.

Himself."[1] "We know that when He shall appear, we shall be like Him, for we shall see Him as He is."[2] This last expression, doubtless, as many assert, refers to a spiritual conformity to Christ, which shall be perfected when we come into His immediate presence and into full intimacy. Even this would necessitate also an outward resemblance to His person, for the external is, as we have seen, the manifestation of the internal. But the interpretation can not be restricted to change in character. We are now made like Him in graces. At death we are to be made perfect in holiness. The text speaks of a resemblance "which doth not yet appear." It promises that "He shall appear" again. His return in the flesh was the constant hope of the early disciples. We shall then "see Him as He is," in all His external and bodily

[1] Phil. iii. 20, 21.   [2] I John iii. 2.

glory, as well as in divine perfections. And when we shall thus "see the King in His beauty,"[1] "we shall be like Him," as we rise to meet Him in the air.

Let us therefore consider the glorious body of Christ as the "first fruits" of the resurrection. It was material and had all the functions of the body. It could be "handled," "held by the feet." Thomas could put his finger in the print of the nails and thrust his hand into His side. "Behold My hands and My feet that it is I Myself, handle Me and see, for a spirit hath not flesh and bones as ye see Me have."[2] He could touch His disciples, walk to Emmaus, take bread, bless and break it and give it to them. He could eat "a piece of a broiled fish and of a honeycomb."[3] "He breathed upon them,"[4] and

[1] Is. xxxiii. 17.
[2] Luke xxiv. 39.
[3] Luke xxiv. 42.
[4] John xx. 22.

"lifted up His hands and blessed them."[1] It is true that Mary did not at first recognize Him. But it was "early, when it was yet dark."[2] She was in great distress, believing that the dead body of her Master had been stolen. Her eyes were full of tears. She saw Him "as she turned herself back." But she had no thought that He was a spirit. "She supposed He was the gardener." When she really looked at Him, recognition was immediate and full.[2] There was nothing strange in His appearance, manner, or voice. It is also true that the seven disciples at the sea of Tiberias "knew not that it was Jesus." But it was in the early dawn, they were in their boats, having "that night caught nothing." "They were two hundred cubits" from land, and "Jesus stood on the shore." John did soon recognize Him—"It is the Lord"

[1] Luke xxiv. 50. [2] John xx. 1-14.

—and Peter did not hesitate. When they landed, "none o the disciples durst ask Him, Who art thou? Knowing it was the Lord."[1] There was nothing unnatural or unusual in His appearance. And the two who went to Emmaus, when He joined them, thought Him "a stranger in Jerusalem." It is distinctly stated that "their eyes were holden that they should not know Him," and that this continued until He brake the bread, "and their eyes were opened and they knew him."[2] In all other cases the women and the disciples recognized Him at once. It is evident then that Christ had the same body, unaltered in appearance, with the same personal peculiarities and powers as before the crucifixion.

There are other facts which reveal that He possessed new and spiritual characteristics. He "appeared" unto His disciples, and He

[1] John xxi. 4-12.   [2] Luke xxiv. 15-32.

vanished out of their sight. The doors, closed for fear of the Jews, could not exclude Him, nor retain Him. He did not need to walk to Emmaus, for He returned to Jerusalem more rapidly, and appeared to Simon. He ate fish and honey, to satisfy His disciples, and not because he needed earthly food. He was free from the infirmities, necessities and limitations of the body. He possessed new powers and resources. He seems to have spent a greater part of those forty days elsewhere than on earth. This was no longer His abode. Only at times He "appeared," and soon disappeared. At last, while he was speaking, "He was taken up, and a cloud received Him out of their sight, and while they looked steadfastly toward heaven, as He went up, behold two men stood by them in white apparel, which also said, " Ye men of Galilee, why stand ye gazing up into heaven ?

This same Jesus which is taken up from you into heaven, shall so come in like manner as ye have seen Him go into heaven."[1] This same Jesus, " with this spiritual body," " glorious body," now sits at the right hand of the Father, and will come again and call us from our graves, changed after the same image, to be forever with the Lord.

His was therefore a true body, perfectly adapted to come in contact with men in the flesh and with material objects, and as perfectly adapted to the spiritual liberty and state, and to His most glorious exaltation on the throne of His Father. We shall be like Him, when from the graves we shall meet Him in the air, be admitted to the new Jerusalem, and range through the new heavens and the new earth. As there was no difficulty in recognizing Christ after His resurrec-

[1] Acts i. 9-11.

tion, there will be no hesitation in friend greeting friend when we gather, fully redeemed, around the great white throne of our Elder Brother. The same means of recognition which we have already considered, will be even more effectual, and our communion with each other and all saints shall be perfect, and "we shall be satisfied, when we awake with His likeness."[1] (Hebrew, "form.")

[1] Ps. xvii. 15

XIII.

CONCLUSION.

THE comfort to be derived from the recognition of souls after death is inexpressibly great. The forms of our friends are very dear to us. With them they are always associated, and through them we have learned their characters and feelings, and have held sweet converse. We cannot conceive of recognition without the appearance of these same loved forms. We are loath to commit them to the earth, and could scarcely bear the grief if the separation were to be perpetual. Indeed, in every affliction we look for consolation in three directions. We bow in humble submission to the wise and loving will of God. "Not my will but Thine be done."[1] "It is the Lord, let Him do as seemeth Him good."[2] We realize the rest into which our loved one has entered, his freedom from sin and suffering, and his enjoyment of all that Christ has in reserve for His own. And by faith we appropriate and apply to our dead Christ's words, "A little while and we shall not see him, and again a little while and we shall see him,"[3] and David's, "I shall go to Him."[4] These three sources of consolation are really one. We recognize the love which has determined our purification by sorrow, and the perfecting of our departed one in glory, and we are eager to share the present and eternal blessedness with him and the Lord. Heaven seems more our home, as

[1] Luke xxii. 42.   [2] I Sam. iii. 18.
[3] John xvi. 16.   [4] II Sam. xii. 23.

the members of our family there gather, and much of its happiness shall consist in renewed association, which shall never again be disturbed. All this has been suggested in the preceding pages, and needs not to be enlarged upon.

The doctrine justifies the care which we naturally take of our bodies. Their highest value is, as the Scriptures tell us, that they are the temples of the Holy Ghost, and we are exhorted therefore not to defile them with sin or worldliness, but to keep their members pure for God's worship and service. "If any man defile the temple of God, him shall God destroy, for the temple of God is holy, which temple ye are."[1] But this exhortation is further enforced by the fact that our bodies and their characteristics of form and feature are an essential part of our persons,

[1] I Cor. iii. 17.

and have been redeemed and are to be made perfect, even as our souls. Their organs have been consecrated to the service of Christ and must not be polluted. " With the tongue bless we God, even the Father! and therewith curse we men, which are made after the similitude of God! Out of the same mouth proceedeth blessing and cursing! My brethren, these things ought not so to be."[1] " Know you not that your bodies are the members of Christ? Shall I then take the members of Christ and make them the members of an harlot? God forbid."[2] " We must yield ourselves unto God and our members as instruments of righteousness unto God."[3]

Our forms and features are not of temporary importance but of permanent value. They are not as a scaffold which is to be discarded when the building is erected. We are to be

[1] James iii. 9, 10. [2] I Cor. vi. 15. [3] Rom. vi. 13.

ever associated with them. In them we are to live, by them we are to know and to be known, and through them we are to operate forever, praising God and blessing others. We ought, therefore, to guard their beauty, develop their powers, and see that they always truly represent our real characters and reveal the grace which we have received from Christ. All should "take knowledge of us that we have been with Jesus."[1] For the same reason we should be careful of the features of others, lightening their countenances, and rejoicing in their spiritual beauty and conformity to the image of Christ.

Abraham bought a field and a cave for a possession of a burying place, and there buried his dead.[2] Jacob charged his sons, "I am to be gathered unto my people: bury me with my fathers."[3] The sepul-

[1] Acts iv. 13.　　[2] Gen. xxiii. 20.　　[3] Gen. xlix. 29.

chres were guarded with care, as was that of David, for many generations. "God buried Moses in the valley in the land of Moab,"[1] and "Michael the archangel, contending with the devil, disputed about the body of Moses."[2] And angels sat on the stone, and "at the head and at the feet where the body of Jesus had lain."[3] It is right, therefore, to respect the resting places of those that sleep. Their bodies must see corruption, but they are precious and shall come forth again with new beauty to die no more. Christ did not reprove the Scribes and Pharisees because "they built the tombs of the prophets and garnished the sepulchres of the righteous"; but because while doing so they were like their fathers, persecuting those of whom the prophets and righteous men had spoken, and were "filling up the measure of their

[1] Deut. xxxiv. 6. [2] Jude, 9. [3] John xx. 12.

fathers."[1] He Himself said of His friend, "Where have ye laid him?" And "Jesus wept"[2] when He came to the grave. The places are holy where the bodies of saints await the resurrection and are often called "God's acres." They should be kept beautiful, adorned with the emblems of immortality.

Some may find a tendency to idolatry in the decoration of graves, as an offering of reverence to the bodies and ascribing a virtue to the bones. But sin finds occasion to sin in all things. The act itself is holy. We surround the tomb with symbols of our faith that the end is not yet, that though these bodies have returned to the dust, they shall come forth again, and that the resurrection is a certainty, which we are eagerly anticipating.

The custom of cremation, which some are

[1] Matt. xxiii. 29-32.   [2] John xi. 34, 35.

introducing, is anti-Christian, notwithstanding the arguments which may be educed in its favor. It has no countenance in Scripture. The bodies of Saul and of his sons were burnt by the valiant men of Jabesh-gilead. But they had been mutilated and long exposed, and were probably burnt to prevent further desecration by the Philistines. "Their bones were buried under a tree at Jabesh."[1] Amos speaks of the burning of those who died in a plague, and probably for that reason.[2] The early church denounced it as a heathen custom, as dishonoring the body and suggesting the denial of the resurrection. Many who now advocate cremation have no faith in the literal rising of the dead, and not a few discard Christianity. In Scripture fire is the type of destruction, complete and without remedy, the condemnation due for sin.

[1] I Sam. xxxi. 11-13.   [2] Amos vi. 10.

This is true even when purification by fire is spoken of. The gold is not injured, but its impurities are burnt. The Christian is defiled with sin, which afflictions cause him to perceive and hate. The sin shall be entirely removed and the tried saint perfected. In sacrifices the animal was regarded as bearing the transgressions of the people, and, being under condemnation, it was consumed from the altar. In a few cases the bodies of criminals were burnt, to indicate the greatness of their sin and the unending character of their punishment. "And Joshua said, Why hast thou troubled us? The Lord shall trouble thee this day. And all Israel stoned him with stones, and burned them with fire, after they had stoned them with stones, and they raised over him a great heap of stones unto this day."[1] Cremation, therefore, signifies a

[1] Joshua vii. 25, 26.

denial of the resurrection, and that the body is irredeemably under the curse of sin. Burial is in hope of the resurrection, in faith in the redemption of the body, and in love for those whom we shall see again with the Lord.

There is another precious thought involved in the recognition after death. We have an instinctive desire to see our loved ones, and prophets and righteous men essentially as they were while on earth. To be assured of their identity and to hold sweet converse on eternal things would only half satisfy us, if as to appearance and personal characteristics they are to have no connection with their earthly lives. The brethren of Joseph found no pleasure in him, the Egyptian, the second ruler of the land, although thus he was able to feed and to advance them. But with joy they greeted him, when as a son "he fell on his father's neck, and wept on his neck a good while," and when he was not ashamed to acknowledge their trade as shepherds, though "every shepherd is an abomination unto the Egyptians."[1] In heaven we shall find not merely glorified saints, bearing the names of those who once lived on earth, but men, identified with earthly histories, sanctified. We shall not wonder how this Abraham could ever have been a stranger and pilgrim in the land, paid tithes to Melchisedek, offered up his son Isaac, and been called the father of faithful. His very person will bring all these scenes before us. Moses will appear as when he stood before Pharaoh, divided the Red Sea, came down from Sinai with his face shining with glory, and as he stood on Pisgah and viewed the promised land. David will be the sweet

[1] Gen. xlvi. 29-34.

singer of Israel, and Elijah, Isaiah, Daniel and all the prophets will recall to us their past trials as they forever foretell future glory. We long to see each of the apostles individualized and associated with gospel scenes. And so with later saints and personal friends. Remembered histories will possess new charms in the midst of the actors who taught, suffered, fought and died for the precious faith.

To see Christ in His glory will be rapture indeed. But still greater will be the joy of beholding that He retains His humanity, the very body that bore our sins on the tree, "the Lamb as it had been slain,"[1] wounded for our redemption. We are often troubled because even faith cannot draw His features, nor imagine how He appeared in the flesh when He went in and out among men. But we

[1] Rev. v. 6.

shall be gratified. We shall see what attracted the twelve, gave Peter his boldness, drew forth John's love, excited the faith of sufferers, encouraged the timid and brought sinners to his feet. His delight in His Father's work, interest in His doctrine, His pity for the ignorant and love for His own shall be witnessed by us. We shall see Jesus, and realize what He was, and is, and ever shall be, the SON OF MAN. And we shall perceive, what now we cannot, how fully He has also entered into all the experiences though which we have passed, and by which He has brought us to glory.

www.ingramcontent.com/pod-product-compliance
Lightning Source LLC
Chambersburg PA
CBHW031445160426
43195CB00010BB/860